Best Easy Day Hikes
Rhode Island

Help Us Keep This Guide Up to Date

Every effort has been made by the author and editors to make this guide as accurate and useful as possible. However, many things can change after a guide is published—trails are rerouted, regulations change, techniques evolve, facilities come under new management, etc.

We appreciate hearing from you concerning your experiences with this guide and how you feel it could be improved and kept up to date. While we may not be able to respond to all comments and suggestions, we'll take them to heart and we'll also make certain to share them with the author. Please send your comments and suggestions to the following address:

Globe Pequot Press
Reader Response/Editorial Department
246 Goose Lane, Suite 200
Guilford, CT 06437

Thanks for your input, and happy trails!

Best Easy Day Hikes Series

Best Easy Day Hikes
Rhode Island

Second Edition

Steve Mirsky

Revised by James Buchanan

FALCONGUIDES

GUILFORD, CONNECTICUT

FALCONGUIDES®

An imprint of Globe Pequot, the trade division of
The Rowman & Littlefield Publishing Group, Inc.
4501 Forbes Blvd., Ste. 200
Lanham, MD 20706
www.rowman.com

Falcon and FalconGuides are registered trademarks and Make Adventure Your Story is a trademark of The Rowman & Littlefield Publishing Group, Inc.

Distributed by NATIONAL BOOK NETWORK

Copyright © 2010, 2022 The Rowman & Littlefield Publishing Group, Inc.

Maps by The Rowman & Littlefield Publishing Group, Inc.

British Library Cataloguing in Publication Information available

Library of Congress Cataloging-in-Publication Data
Name: Mirsky, Steve, 1972–, author.
Title: Best easy day hikes Rhode Island / Steve Mirsky ; Revised by James
    Buchanan.
Description: Second edition. | Lanham : Globe Pequot, [2022] | Series: Best
    easy day hikes series | Summary: "Discover up-to-date, expert-tested easy
    hikes for every skill level in the Rhode Island area! Great for families, day
    hikers, transplants and tourists, Best Easy Day Hikes Rhode Island, Second
    Edition includes concise descriptions and detailed maps for the best
    accessible and scenic hikes in Rhode Island"—Provided by publisher.
Identifiers: LCCN 2021036230 (print) | LCCN 2021036231 (ebook) | ISBN
    9781493046140 (paperback) | ISBN 9781493046157 (epub)
Subjects: LCSH: Hiking—Rhode Island—Guidebooks. | Trails—Rhode Island—
    Guidebooks. | Rhode Island—Guidebooks.
Classification: LCC GV199.42.R4 M57 2022 (print) | LCC GV199.42.R4
    (ebook) | DDC 796.5109745—dc23
LC record available at https://lccn.loc.gov/2021036230
LC ebook record available at https://lccn.loc.gov/20210362310

♾™ The paper used in this publication meets the minimum requirements of American National Standard for Information Sciences—Permanence of Paper for Printed Library Materials, ANSI/NISO Z39.48-1992.

Contents

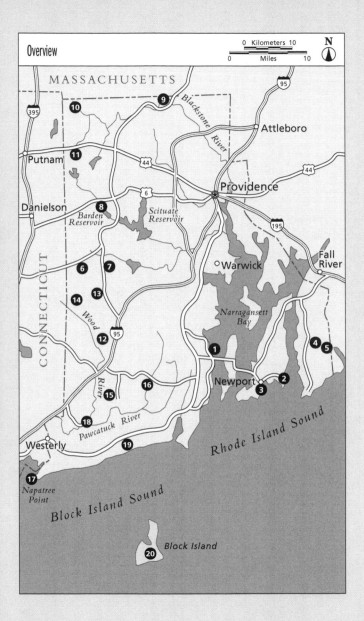

Acknowledgments

I am indebted to the countless volunteers who maintain trails throughout the state of Rhode Island, whether they are blue-blazed trails spanning multiple counties or shorter quasi-public systems. Their efforts, along with those of individuals who have had the foresight to preserve open space even in the face of extreme development pressures, make many routes in this guidebook possible.

Thanks to the expert team of editors and production staff at Rowman & Littlefield for helping me make the second edition of this guide the best it can be. Special thanks to my wife, Renee, who supported my time away on weekends to cover these hikes and my long periods buried behind my laptop typing up these chapters.

Meet Your Guides

Steve Mirsky, the author, is an avid outdoorsman who has lived in New England for most of his life. He's hiked New Hampshire's Mount Washington in the winter, portions of the Long Trail in Vermont, and many a bend, overlook, and rock outcropping on trails throughout the Nutmeg State. Steve says he has a special fondness for Rhode Island's remarkably diverse terrain. Steve has over three years' experience as a freelance writer of destination features and has written articles for numerous publications, including *American Forests* magazine and GoNomad.com. He regularly covers food and culture on his blog at gastrotraveling.com and is also a regular blogger for planeteyetraveler.com, covering the latest local news, restaurant reviews, and unique cultural offerings in New York City. Other articles have covered Brooklyn's "Boro Park," the country's largest Orthodox Jewish neighborhood, and "The International Express," a diverse conglomeration of neighborhoods in Queens, as well as Long Island's North Fork and the Hamptons.

James Buchanan, the reviser, is a fiftyish journalist, writing coach, and outdoors writer living in the Seacoast region of New Hampshire with his family. He has worked for the Forest Service and traveled extensively throughout the United States. He attended Quaker schools, and his first love has always been storytelling. In addition to his own writing, he is a ghostwriter of memoirs and creative nonfiction and an editor who helps people create high-quality and salable manuscripts. His work has won multiple awards, and several are in the process of being adapted to the screen. James loves to hike and get into nature as much as possible. His website is www.orchardwriting.com.

Introduction

This small pocket guide contains twenty day hikes, ranging in length from 1 to 5 miles approximately, covering the diverse landscape within the small state of Rhode Island. No more than an hour's drive from South County to the eastern shore of the Sakonnet River to the vast Arcadia Management Area near the western border, Rhode Island's terrain represents an easy-to-reach microcosm of all that southern New England's outdoors has to offer. Some trails are well marked and heavily used while others are difficult to locate without referring to the following hike descriptions. Beaches and marshes, rock-encrusted mountainsides, and easygoing wood roads are all covered here. Whether you want to simply beachcomb for a couple of hours, enjoy lakeside vistas from beneath a canopy of cedars, or do some ridge-walking for panoramic views, *Best Easy Day Hikes Rhode Island* covers the best places to escape civilization for a while, all less than an hour's drive from Providence's vibrant urban living. This is the Ocean State; you will experience the salty air and deep blue coastal waters of Rhode Island firsthand on some of these routes, and these qualities are palpable on the rest.

The Nature of Rhode Island

Rhode Island's hiking grounds range from rugged, steep climbs to flat, wide-open beaches to miles of wood roads once heavily used for commerce. Hikes in this guide cover the gamut. While by definition a best easy day hike is not strenuous and generally poses little danger to the traveler, knowing a few details about nature in Rhode Island will enhance your explorations.

1

Weather

Rhode Island weather varies greatly depending on the season. Even though the climate is more temperate here than anywhere else in New England, there are still periods of unpredictability, which is synonymous with weather patterns in the Northeast. Winter temperatures can dip below zero for a handful of days, aided by a windchill, but the average temperature between December and February is 30 degrees. From June through August, temperatures typically average in the 70s. Periods of humidity during the summer can spike to uncomfortable levels without warning, while winter precipitation can range from freezing rain to snow within the same day.

Because of this relative unpredictability, trail conditions can change greatly from day to day. However, you will be well prepared for winter hiking by following these rules of thumb: Layer up in winter with a breathable long-sleeved shirt, fleece pullover, and then a waterproof coat as an outer layer. Depending on whether trails are covered with deep or packed snow or ice, either waterproof boots with gaiters and snowshoes or waterproof hiking boots outfitted with ice grippers will serve you well.

Spring (March through May) tends to be wet, muddy at times, and increasingly buggy beginning in April. Wear your bug repellent, a breathable T-shirt, a sweatshirt, and a windbreaker, along with waterproof hiking boots. In summer (June through August), a T-shirt, shorts, liberally applied insect repellent, and plenty of water will keep you comfortable.

My favorite hiking season is fall (September through November). The mosquitoes and gnats are gone, foliage is starting to turn colors, and blue skies with periods of warm, bright sun and cool breezes make hiking a joy. The only downside is that thousands of others likely feel the same way, so you may have company en route.

Critters

You'll encounter mostly benign creatures on these trails, such as deer, squirrels, chipmunks, wild turkeys, and a variety of songbirds and shorebirds. More rarely seen (during the daylight hours especially) are coyotes, raccoons, and opossums. Deer in some of the parks are remarkably tame and may linger on or close to the trail as you approach.

While rare, Rhode Island's preserves and parks may also be home to black bears, copperheads, and rattlesnakes. Encounters are infrequent, but you should be prepared to react properly if you run across a dangerous snake, a bear, or a rabid nocturnal animal such as a raccoon or opossum.

Snakes generally strike only if threatened. You are too big to be dinner, so they typically avoid contact with humans. Keep your distance, and they will keep theirs. If you come across a bear, make yourself as big as possible and do not run. If you don't act like or look like prey, you stand a good chance of not being attacked. Warning them ahead of time by wearing a bell helps to avoid contact in the first place.

And if you encounter an animal normally seen at night, especially if it has matted fur and foam on its mouth, steer clear of it. If necessary, turn back and postpone your hike. Rabid animals can't be reasoned with and should never be approached or fed.

Be Prepared

Hiking in Rhode Island is generally safe. Still, hikers should be prepared, whether they are out for an easy stroll to

Napatree Point or ridge-walking through Carolina South. Some specific advice:

- Know the basics of first aid, including how to treat bleeding, bites and stings, and fractures, strains, or sprains. Pack a first-aid kit on each excursion.

- Familiarize yourself with the symptoms of heat exhaustion, heat stroke, and hypothermia. Heat exhaustion symptoms include heavy sweating, muscle cramps, headache, dizziness, and fainting. Should you or any of your hiking party exhibit any of these symptoms, cool the victim down immediately by rehydrating and getting him or her to an air-conditioned location. Cold showers also help reduce body temperature. Heatstroke is much more serious: the victim may lose consciousness and the skin is hot and dry to the touch. In this event, call 911 immediately. Hypothermia does not require exposure to subzero temperatures. Even damp, relatively mild weather can make you susceptible—any condition that brings your body temperature below 95 degrees. Symptoms include uncontrollable shivering, confusion, and pale, cold skin. Treat mild symptoms by removing wet clothing and replacing with dry layers, drinking hot liquids, eating a highly sugared snack, and maintaining movement to maximize blood flow. If conditions worsen, seek medical help immediately.

- Regardless of the weather, your body needs a lot of water while hiking. A full 32-ounce bottle is the minimum for these short hikes, but more is always better. Bring a full water bottle, whether water is available along the trail or not.

- Don't drink from streams, rivers, creeks, or lakes without treating or filtering the water first. Waterways and water bodies may host a variety of contaminants including bacteria, which can cause serious intestinal unrest.
- Prepare for extremes of both heat and cold by dressing in layers.
- Carry a backpack in which you can store extra clothing, ample drinking water and food, and whatever goodies, like guidebooks, cameras, and binoculars, you might want.
- Most area trails have cell phone coverage. Bring your device, but make sure you've turned it off or got it on the vibrate setting while hiking. Nothing like a "wake the dead"–loud ring to startle every creature, including fellow hikers.
- Keep children under careful watch. Hazards along some of the trails include poison oak and ivy, uneven footing, and steep drop-offs; make sure children don't stray from the designated route. Children should carry a plastic whistle; if they become lost, they should stay in one place and blow the whistle to summon help.

Zero Impact

Many trails in Rhode Island are heavily used year-round. We, as trail users and advocates, must be especially vigilant to make sure our passage leaves no lasting mark. Here are some basic guidelines for preserving trails in the region:

- Pack out all your own trash, including biodegradable items like orange peels. You might also pack out garbage left by less considerate hikers.

- Don't approach or feed any wild creatures—the ground squirrel eyeing your snack food is best able to survive if it remains self-reliant.

- Don't pick wildflowers or gather rocks, antlers, feathers, and other treasures along the trail. Removing these items will only take away from the next hiker's experience.

- Avoid damaging trailside soils and plants by remaining on the established route. This is also a good rule of thumb for avoiding poison oak and ivy.

- Don't cut switchbacks, which can promote erosion.

- Be courteous by not making loud noises while hiking.

- Some of these trails are multiuse, which means you'll share them with other hikers, trail runners, mountain bikers, and possibly equestrians. Familiarize yourself with the proper trail etiquette, yielding the trail when appropriate.

- Use outhouses at trailheads or along the trail.

Rhode Island Corridors

Since Rhode Island is the smallest state in the United States, all hikes are roughly an hour or less from Providence. Each hike in this guidebook is also no more than an hour from all the others.

Major routes referenced within the guide include I-95 (north–south), and state routes 6 (east–west), 44 (east–west), 1 (north–south), 138 (east–west), and 114 (north–south).

Land Management

The following government and private organizations manage most of the public lands described in this guide and can provide further information on these hikes and other trails in their service areas, though it should be noted that few of these contacts are open on weekends or provide complete maps, updates, and information. There are, however, well-maintained websites (such as AllTrails.com) and apps (such as Gaia GPS) that provide detailed maps and trail updates.

- State of Rhode Island Department of Environmental Management (DEM)—Division of Parks & Recreation Headquarters, 1100 Tower Hill Rd., North Kingstown, RI 02852; (401) 667-6200; www.riparks.com
- U.S. Fish and Wildlife Service—Rhode Island National Wildlife Refuge (NWR) Complex, 50 Bend Rd., Charlestown, RI 02813; (401) 364-9124; www.fws.gov/ refuge/Ninigret/About_the_Complex
- Cliff Walk Commission—City of Newport, 43 Broadway, Newport, RI 02840; (401) 845-5300; www.cliff walk.com
- Town of Tiverton Open Space Commission, 343 Highland Rd., Tiverton, RI 02878; (401) 625-6700; www .tiverton.ri.gov/boards/conservation.php
- Audubon Society of Rhode Island, 12 Sanderson Rd., Smithfield, RI 02917; (401) 949-5454; audubon@asri .org
- Town of Foster, 181 Howard Hill Rd., Foster, RI 02825; (401) 392 9200; www.townoffoster.com
- Department of Conservation and Recreation, 251 Causeway St., Suite 600, Boston, MA 02114-2104; (617) 626-1250; mass.parks@state.ma.us; www.mass.gov/dcr/
- Watch Hill Fire District, 222 Watch Hill Rd., Westerly, RI 02891; (401) 348-6540; www.watchhillfiredistrict .org

- The Nature Conservancy, Rhode Island Chapter, 159 Waterman St., Providence, RI 02906; (401) 331-7110; www.nature.org; ri@tnc.org

Public Transportation

Access to most of these hikes is by car. Rhode Island Public Transit Authority (RIPTA) is the only exposure you'll get to public transportation along these routes. Contact RIPTA at 265 Melrose St., Providence, RI 02907; (401) 781-9400; www.ripta.com.

How to Use This Guide

This guide is designed to be simple and easy to use. Each hike is described with a map and summary information that delivers the trail's vital statistics including length, difficulty, elevation gain (low point to high point), fees and permits, park hours, canine compatibility, and trail contacts. Directions to the trailhead are also provided, along with a general description of what you'll see along the way. A detailed route finder (Miles and Directions) sets forth mileages between significant landmarks along the trail.

It should also be noted that the organizations that manage the various trails may be difficult to get ahold of, especially on weekends, and that their websites often do not include maps or current conditions and information. For this reason, you may prefer to find maps and current conditions on sites such as AllTrails.com or via cell phone apps such as Gaia GPS.

Further, trail mileages are notoriously variable depending on the technology used. For this guide, we used the Gaia GPS cell phone app, which comes with several handy features, includes maps of many of the trails in this guide, and can be used just about anywhere.

Hike Selection

This guide describes trails that are accessible to every hiker, whether visiting from out of town or a longtime resident of Rhode Island. Most hikes are no longer than 5 miles round trip, and some are considerably shorter. They range in difficulty from flat excursions perfect for a family outing to more challenging treks in the more extensive state parks. While these trails are among the best, keep in mind that nearby trails, often in the same park or preserve, may offer options better suited to your needs.

Difficulty Ratings

These are all easy hikes, but easy is a relative term. Some would argue that no hike involving any kind of climbing is easy, but here in southern New England hills are everywhere—although not usually prolonged. To aid in the selection of a hike that suits particular needs and abilities, each is rated easy or moderate. Bear in mind that even more challenging routes can be made easy by hiking within your limits and taking rests when you need them.

Easy hikes are generally short and flat, most taking one to two hours to complete.

Moderate hikes involve increased distance and relatively mild changes in elevation, and generally will take between two and three and a half hours to complete.

These are completely subjective ratings—consider that what you think is easy is entirely dependent on your level of fitness and the adequacy of your gear (primarily shoes). If you are hiking with a group, you should select a hike with a rating that's appropriate for the least fit and prepared in your party.

Approximate hiking times are based on the assumption that on flat ground, most walkers average two miles per hour. Adjust that rate by the steepness of the terrain and your level of fitness (subtract time if you're an aerobic animal and add time if you're hiking with kids), and you have a ballpark hiking duration. Be sure to add more time if you plan to picnic or take part in other activities like bird-watching or photography.

Trail Finder

Best Hikes for River Lovers

Best Hikes for Lake Lovers

Best Hikes for Children

Best Hikes for Dogs

Best Hikes for Great Views

Best Hikes for Nature Lovers

Best Hikes for History Buffs

Map Legend

══════╣95╠══════	Interstate Highway
─────╣44╠─────	U.S. Highway
═════(117)═════	State Highway
─────────────	Local Road
▬▬▬▬▬▬▬▬▬	Featured Trail
-------------	Trail
┝━┿━┿━┿━┥	Railroad
─ ─ ─·─ ─ ─··	State Line
～～～～～～	River/Creek
⸺⸺⸺	Marsh/Swamp
≋	Boat Launch
⌣	Bridge
⊛	Capital
•—•	Gate
❷	Information Center
🅿	Parking
▲	Peak
■	Point of Interest/Structure
○	Town
⓫	Trailhead
▧	Viewpoint/Overlook
≩	Waterfall

1 John H. Chafee Nature Preserve

This hike takes you out to Rome Point, the most reliable spot on Narragansett Bay for viewing seals between October and May. Terrain on the first leg of this route is a flat pebbled access road straight out to the beach. Then, after some beach walking, you'll head out to the point through a cedar grove with water views on either side. The return route passes through a wooded marsh past remains of an old farmstead ripe for exploration.

Distance: 2.5-mile lollipop
Approximate hiking time: 1 hour
Difficulty: Easy
Elevation gain: 80 feet
Trail surface: Gravel road, wooded trail
Best season: Oct–Apr for seal viewing
Other trail users: Cross-country skiers
Canine compatibility: Dogs must be on leash at all times

Permits and fees: None
Schedule: Open year-round from sunrise to sunset
Maps: TOPO! New England; trail maps at signboard near trailhead
Trail contact: State of Rhode Island DEM—Division of Parks & Recreation Headquarters, 1100 Tower Hill Rd., North Kingstown, RI 02852; (401) 667-6200; www .riparks.com

Finding the trailhead: From Providence and points north, take RI 1A through historic Wickford into the village of Hamilton. The trail entrance and parking will be 1.5 miles south of Hamilton to your left (east) and is marked with signage.

From the south, the trailhead is to your right (east) just over 0.5 mile on Route 1A from the intersection of RI 138. You'll know you've gone too far if you pass a brown sign with white lettering advertising the GILBERT STUART MUSEUM to the left (west).

The Hike

From the dirt parking lot surrounded by low-lying thick wooden railings, the trail begins on a gravel access road marked with a commemorative plaque and covered signboard containing a trail map to your right. The road is very straight and flat after a slight decline from the parking area. Wooded marsh surrounds a sand and gravel roadbed elevated from the wetness. Your return trail comes in from the right, but it's not readily visible. Continue straight.

A plain scrubby forest consisting of swamp maples and dense undergrowth grows to your left (north) and marsh continues on the right (south). Stone walls and a drier forest floor become visible through the trees. You'll notice side trails cutting into the woods to your left, but stay straight on the main road.

A power line crosses the road at 0.4 mile; here you'll walk down a slight grade as you curve to the left. This is notable since up to this point the trail was completely flat and straight for as far as the eye could see. You'll reach the intersection of several trails at about 0.6 mile, where another power line crosses overhead. A narrow footpath leads into the woods to your right (south), and a grassy access road paralleling the power line begins to your left (north). Continue straight on the access road toward the ocean, which you can now see in the distance through the trees.

After passing the convergence of trails, you'll pass a modest cedar grove to your left (north). At the coastline, you'll be on Narragansett Bay with the Jamestown Bridge in the distance to your right (south). Turn left (northeast), walking along the beach, which is a mix of gravelly stone and sand with brushy woods fronting the shoreline to your left (west).

This may not be a sunbathing or swimming beach, but it certainly has picturesque bay and island views.

Soon you'll see a marsh behind the beach head to your left. A ways past the marsh, at about the 1.0-mile mark, you'll see a trail to your left (west) marked by a small rock pile beneath a cedar. Take this trail—though, you can continue along the beach out to the point if you like—and join a narrow sandy trail, walking down a narrow peninsula to Rome Point. Tidal estuary waters are to your left (west), and the open bay is to your right (east) through dense cedar groves.

The trail is flat at sea level, and at 1.2 miles, you'll reach the tip of Rome Point, which is the best vantage point for seal watching. As you look straight out into the bay, you'll see small rocks poking up above the waterline where the seals hang out, and also notice a larger island with a house to the left (northeast) of these rocks. Turn around and retrace your steps or explore some side trails that spider off the main trail to your right (west) to the water's edge. There's not much room to deviate, and soon the side trails parallel and connect back to the main trail. Bright white shells, dark stones on the shore, the blue ocean, and dark green cedars all envelop you, along with the ocean breezes, making it a memorable spot.

Once you reach the peninsula's base at about 1.4 miles, continue straight ahead on the footpath heading west, instead of veering left back down to the beach. Now the tidal estuary will be immediately to your right (north), visible through the cedars and down a small bank. This leg of the route gives you a different perspective of the estuary, with the wide-open bay in the distance. Views can, at times, be industrial in the distance but overall, they are still picturesque.

You'll enter a thick cedar grove at 1.5 miles, moving away from the water even though it remains visible to your right (north) through the trees. Winding into the interior of woods with more swamp maples in the mix, the trail bed is now carved down into the forest floor about 6 inches with a straight edge on either side, giving it the appearance of an old wagon road. It's obvious that traffic other than pedestrians predominated here at one time.

An intersection at 1.6 miles marks a trail to the left (south), but continue straight (southwest) through cedars mixed with saplings. Stay on the main trail even though you'll see narrow footpaths branching out to the left.

As you reach a power line at 1.8 miles, cross beneath the power line and reenter the woods. Shortly after you reenter the woods, an old, rusted car from the 1950s will be visible through the trees to your left (south); continue straight on the main trail. From here, you will essentially follow this main trail back to where it intersects with the main access road you came in on from the parking area.

The forest mix broadens with some midgrowth oak, swamp maple, and a few cedars. Soon, through the trees to your right (northwest), you'll see a deep and steep cellar hole. You will then come upon a shallow gully that parallels the trail until you reach a stone wall to the left (west) fronting a small marsh filled with water. At about the 2.0-mile mark, this marsh drains via a small stream under the trail and into the gully.

A little beyond this point, you'll see an old homesite with a large concrete foundation, possibly a barn, to your right. A stream flows to the left (west) of the trail, and the path increasingly narrows, surrounded by dense briars and honey-suckle. There will be a number of trails veering off to either direction, but remain on the main trail.

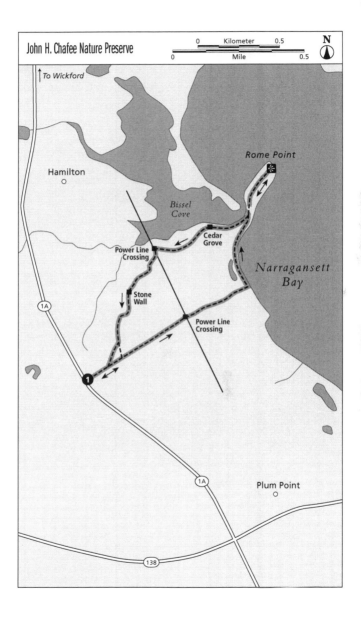

John H. Chafee Nature Preserve

0   Kilometer   0.5
0   Mile   0.5

N

↑ To Wickford

Hamilton
○

Bissel Cove

Rome Point

Cedar Grove

Power Line Crossing

Narragansett Bay

Stone Wall

Power Line Crossing

1A

1

1A

Plum Point
○

138

At 2.3 miles, pass a large rock formation jutting out of the forest floor to your right (west). This is striking since there aren't others like it nearby or on the entire route. Go straight not left at the intersection near here where you'll soon connect back to the flat and straight access road you initially hiked in on. Turn right (west) onto this road and retrace your steps back to the parking area.

Miles and Directions

0.0 Begin at a slight decline from dirt parking lot.

0.4 Curve left down a slight grade under a power line.

0.6 Continue straight (northeast) through the intersection of several trails where the power line crosses overhead.

1.0 Depart the beach to the left marked by a small pile of rocks beneath a cedar and join a sandy trail to Rome Point.

1.2 Reach the tip of Rome Point, the best vantage point for seal watching depending on the season.

1.5 Enter a thick cedar grove with the water still visible through the trees.

1.6 Continue straight (southwest) at the trail intersection.

1.8 Cross underneath the power lines; then pass an old, wrecked car; remain on the main trail.

2.3 Pass a large rock formation; remain on the main trail until it connects with the access road.

2.5 Arrive back at the trailhead.

2 Sachuest Point National Wildlife Refuge

One of five national wildlife refuges in Rhode Island, Sachuest Point was farmland used for sheep grazing into the early 1900s and then was used by the U.S. Navy during World War II as a rifle range and communications center. Thick underbrush and some open meadows remain on this prime 242-acre spit of protected land extending out into the Atlantic Ocean. A key stopover and wintering area for migratory birds, the entire preserve is an ornithologist's dream come true.

Distance: 2.4-mile loop
Approximate hiking time: 1 hour
Difficulty: Easy
Elevation gain: 40 feet
Trail surface: Crushed stone dust
Best season: Sept–Nov and Apr–June for the best bird viewing and fewer crowds
Other trail users: Cross-country skiers, joggers
Canine compatibility: No dogs permitted

Permits and fees: None
Schedule: Open year-round from sunrise to sunset
Maps: TOPO! New England; trail map at visitor center
Trail contact: U.S. Fish and Wildlife Service–Rhode Island NWR Complex, 50 Bend Rd., Charlestown, RI 02813; (401) 364-9124; https://www.fws.gov/refuge/sachuest_point

Finding the trailhead: From the Providence area, take Route 1 south to Middletown; then follow Route 138 east over the Newport Bridge. Take the Newport exit and pass through downtown Newport on Route 138A. Once through the downtown area, you'll pass First (or Newport) Beach. Just past First Beach, turn right (east) onto Purgatory

Road; then turn right (southeast) onto Sachuest Point Road and follow it until it dead-ends at refuge parking lot. Restrooms, water, and
complimentary trail maps at visitor center.

The Hike

Begin by walking on the paved sidewalk along the edge of
the parking lot, with the visitor center to your right (south).
Turn left on the sidewalk, which transitions to crushed stone
as soon as you depart the parking area, passing through a low
wooden railing dividing the parking lot from the trail. A trail
map is posted on a stand ahead.

From the map sign, begin to the left on the Flint Point
Loop Trail, a completely flat, stone-dust surface that remains
consistent throughout the entire route. Turn left (west) at
0.1 mile, through a thick tunnel of dense low-lying briars,
honeysuckle, and scrub brush. The briny air and ever-
present sound of surf crashing in the distance punctuates
the serenity.

The first views of the Sakonnet River are visible at the
0.5-mile mark as you walk toward Flint Point, which juts out
into the wide, bay-like Sakonnet River.

At 0.6 mile, you'll reach Flint Point marked by a wooden
bird-viewing platform to your immediate left (northwest).
The trail makes a sharp right (east) following the contour
of the point, continuing close along the water's edge. At the
0.7-mile mark you will have your first view of the wide
open Atlantic and will have mostly continuous ocean views
with surf pounding against the rugged coastline. Different
minerals in the rocks also produce a wide variety of color,
especially in contrast with the ocean surf and wide-open sky.
Because the trail is so flat and scenic, the terrain is perfect for
jogging and power walking.

Pass another viewing platform close up to the ocean, complete with a telescope that's free to use, at 0.9 mile. This point also marks the spot where you'll be walking away from the Sakonnet River to your left (east), and toward the more open and tumultuous Atlantic Ocean, feeling the ocean's full impact with waves crashing close by and stiff winds. Numerous shore access points are available to your left (southeast), giving you the opportunity to explore various rock formations right on the water's edge.

Continue straight on the Ocean View Loop Trail, hiking through an intersection at 1.1 miles past a trail that branches out to your right (west) heading back to the parking lot. Wide-open ocean views continue close to your left. Another shore access point at 1.4 miles allows you to explore the rocky coast while enjoying particularly spectacular views up and down the shore as you're standing out on a point.

From this point forward, you'll have unimpeded ocean views to your left (south, then west) and also notice that undergrowth no longer flanks the right side of the trail. Instead, an overgrown field, vestiges of farming that once took place here, extends into the distance.

Upon passing a split rail fence to your right (north) at 1.8 miles, you'll notice unusual midsize trees to your right. Some undergrowth will now separate you from the ocean, but overall, this scene projects the feeling of walking through former farmland right on the ocean.

Reach Sachuest Point; then the trail curves to the right (northwest), moving away from the open ocean and along Sachuest Bay to your left (west). Wide-open views continue, although brush reappears to the right (east), with a modest strip of overgrowth separating you from the water's edge to your left. You'll see fishing access points marked with signage

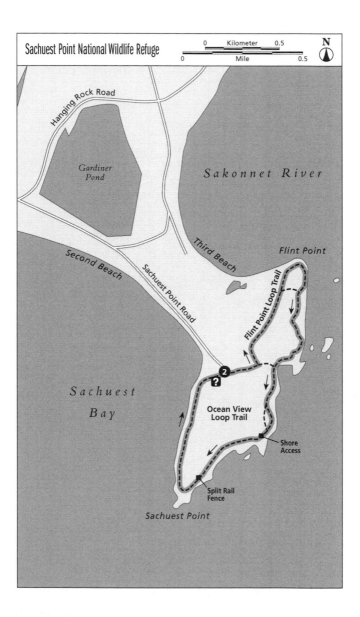

Sachuest Point National Wildlife Refuge

0   Kilometer   0.5

0   Mile   0.5

N

Hanging Rock Road

Gardiner Pond

Sakonnet River

Second Beach

Third Beach

Flint Point

Sachuest Point Road

Flint Point Loop Trail

Sachuest Bay

2

?

Ocean View Loop Trail

Shore Access

Split Rail Fence

Sachuest Point

including a depiction of the different types of fish that can be caught in this area. The visitor center is visible in the distance off to the right (northwest). Continue up to the visitor center, completing the loop back at the parking lot.

Miles and Directions

0.0 Begin on paved sidewalk with the visitor center to your right (south). Take the Flint Point Loop Trail.

0.1 Turn left (west), with the Atlantic Ocean to your left (south).

0.6 Reach the rocky shoreline of Flint Point with a viewing platform to your left (northwest).

0.9 Pass another viewing platform outfitted with a telescope.

1.1 Continue on the Ocean View Loop Trail, passing through an intersection where a trail branches off right (north) to the parking lot.

1.4 Pass a shoreline access point that leads to the water's edge.

1.8 Pass a split rail fence.

2.4 Arrive back at the trailhead.

3 Newport Cliff Walk

Newport's most historic walk passes behind the town's largest mansions, some of them within clear view of the trail. It also has the area's most spectacular ocean vistas, fronting ocean-swept cliffs.

Distance: 3.6 miles point to point (with trolley return)

Approximate hiking time: 2 hours

Difficulty: Moderate

Elevation gain: 38 feet

Trail surface: Concrete sidewalk, crushed stone dust, rock ledge

Best season: Apr–Oct

Other trail users: Joggers

Canine compatibility: Dogs must be on leash at all times

Permits and fees: Small fee to ride the trolley back to the trailhead

Schedule: Open year-round from sunrise to sunset

Maps: TOPO! New England; www .cliffwalk.com

Trail contact: Cliff Walk Commission—City of Newport, 43 Broadway, Newport, RI 02840; (401) 845-5300; www.cliffwalk.com

Finding the trailhead: From the Providence area, take Route 1 south to Middletown; then follow Route 138 east over the Newport Bridge. Take the Newport exit and pass through downtown Newport on Route 138A. Once you pass through the downtown area, drive up a hill on Memorial Boulevard. Parking during summer is extremely challenging, but keep an eye out for spaces available on this boulevard or at Easton's Beach, which is just below the cliff walk entrance. Restrooms and water available at Easton's Beach in summer.

The Hike

The trail begins above Easton's Beach (locally known as First Beach), with wide-open views of this sandy stretch in the distance below to your left (east). Steep cliffs and wide-open ocean views continue to your left (east) as you follow the trail, with the surf breaking in shallow water below for the first 0.5 mile. A large stone wall begins at 0.1 mile, paralleling the trail as you move away from beach cove views. Spectacular mansions provide a free tour of their exteriors, albeit from a distance, along the right (west) side of the trail.

At some points, mansions become obstructed by a fence covered with dense underbrush and briars. Pass a grand overlook terrace marked 40 STEPS at the end of Narragansett Avenue at 0.7 mile. These forty stone steps wind down to a small viewing platform close to the crashing surf. This area provides a historical coastal access point as well as pedestrian egress from the street.

Pass under a small arched bridge as the cliffs become markedly steeper above the crashing waves. Around the corner a 7-foot-tall stone wall runs to your right (west) alongside the trail, and mansion views become apparent, unobstructed by undergrowth. In the distance you will see the campus of Salve Regina University, comprising what were once Gilded Age summer homes.

Continuing with great views, be sure to look back at the jagged coastline that you just walked along. Sometimes it's hard to look back when there is so much to see around the next corner, but don't forget the different perspectives you'll gain by doing this.

Pass through a pair of grand pillars at 1.2 miles, framed with thick and ornate wrought iron gates and fencing to your right (west). Passing through this entry marks a transition from skirting the college grounds to a leveling-off of the trail closer to the water's edge to your left (east). Shortly you'll wind around a small curve, passing stone benches terraced into the cliff that overlook waves continually crashing into the rocks. Aptly named, this spot is the front of the Breakers mansion.

Ruggles Avenue dead-ends into the trail, providing another access point. Here the trail markedly slopes down to the ocean, with mansions in plain view to your right. At the end of this concrete ramp portion of the trail, you'll be directly at the water's edge with a railing separating you from the surf. It's apparent that this section was renovated recently with new concrete and railings.

This enhanced portion abruptly ends at 1.4 miles, where you'll step onto breakwater stones, a radical departure from the previous trail surface. But be sure to continue onward because, even though the trail appears to dissipate into nothingness here, you would be sorely mistaken to turn back.

You'll have clearer views of larger and apparently newer homes immediately to your right. The breakwater continues only for a bit, and then it's back onto an asphalt trail surface. Soon you'll be able to see the Tea House in the distance. At 1.7 miles make an abrupt turn to the right (west), away from and above the water's edge, up onto a concrete surface. It appears that this detour is due to erosion because a chain-link fence straight ahead blocks you from the cliffs and water down below.

Head up along a ridge and pass through a cavernous tunnel underneath the Tea House at 1.9 miles. Even though the Tea House is tantalizingly close, there is no access to the structure from the trail, which can only be accessed from above. In the middle of the tunnel, it gets pretty dark, and there can be puddles depending on the time of year, so exercise caution.

Beyond the tunnel, continue walking south not far above the surf. Rather than steep cliffs separating you from the water, chunks of granite forming a shore-based breakwater prevent erosion and front the water's edge. Particularly on this stretch, you'll realize that the route is filled with multiple vistas and ever-changing views. You'll see coves, rock formations, and the coastline from different angles.

Approach another, shorter, tunnel at 2.1 miles, and as you enter the gloomy passage, you'll get views of the blue ocean directly ahead. The dark blue water framed by sharp rock offers a sharp contrast in color and surroundings. After exiting, pass over breakwater stones and then continue on a crushed stone-dust surface.

Climb down some concrete steps at 2.3 miles onto a rock ledge at sea level. From here until you reach Ledge Road, you'll be cliff-walking on a totally natural surface unaltered by humans except for extremely weathered stone walls that seem to be hundreds of years old. Waves crash into the rocks to your left (west) as you progress on a trail that's rugged and right at wave level. At 2.4 miles reach a great spot where you can sit over a rock outcropping that forms a thunder hole. Waves crashing into the rock crevice underneath emit a loud "boom," and the surf sprays high up onto the cliff, often spraying the edge. Along this stretch a weathered stone wall separates you from the ocean.

Pass over a concrete section of trail for a short distance, still surrounded by rugged terrain. Soon it's back to a rock surface with weathered stone walls on either side. Walk out onto a jetty and look down at waves crashing from the Atlantic Ocean directly into the rock at 2.7 miles. Turn sharply to the right (west) at 2.8 miles, walking along the shore with the direct impact of the Atlantic's wind and waves pounding the rocks and a concrete seawall to your left (south). To your right, several large homes are close by, overlooking the ocean.

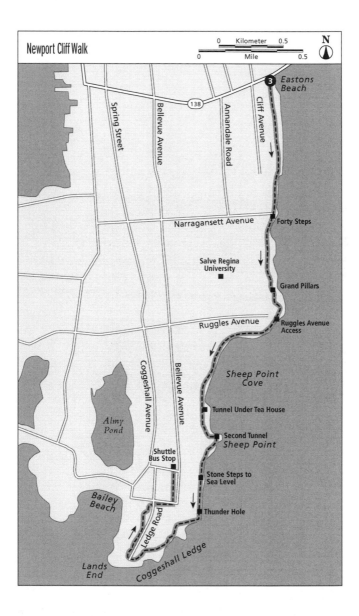

Newport Cliff Walk

0 Kilometer 0.5
0 Mile 0.5

N

Spring Street
Bellevue Avenue
138
Annandale Road
Cliff Avenue

Eastons Beach

Narragansett Avenue
Forty Steps

Salve Regina University

Grand Pillars

Ruggles Avenue
Ruggles Avenue Access

Coggeshall Avenue
Bellevue Avenue

Almy Pond

Sheep Point Cove

Tunnel Under Tea House

Second Tunnel
Sheep Point

Shuttle Bus Stop

Stone Steps to Sea Level

Bailey Beach

Ledge Road

Thunder Hole

Lands End

Coggeshall Ledge

Reach the intersection with Ledge Road at 3 miles, ending your oceanfront walk. To your immediate left, the road dead-ends into the ocean. Turn right (north) onto Ledge Road, take your first right (east) turn onto Bellevue Avenue, and follow Bellevue for several blocks until you see BUS STOP signs for the RIPTA Trolley. Hop on one of these trolleys and ride back to Memorial Boulevard.

Miles and Directions

0.0 Begin on the walkway with wide-open views of Easton's (First) Beach to your left (east).

0.1 Pass a large wall.

0.7 Explore a grand overlook terrace called 40 Steps at the end of Narragansett Avenue.

1.2 Continue through a pair of grand pillars; then pass a trail access point at Ruggles Avenue.

1.4 Step onto breakwater stones.

1.7 Turn abruptly right (west) onto a concrete surface.

1.9 Pass between two stone walls, and pass through a cavernous tunnel underneath the Tea House.

2.1 Enter a second, shorter tunnel with blue ocean views.

2.3 Climb down concrete steps onto a rock at sea level.

2.4 Sit on a rock outcropping that overhangs a thunder hole.

2.7 Walk out onto a jetty and enjoy views of the Atlantic Ocean.

2.8 Turn sharply right (west) toward Ledge Road.

3.0 Turn right (north) onto Ledge Road.

3.6 Arrive at the bus stop and catch a trolley back to the trailhead.

4 Weetamoo Woods– Pardon Gray Preserve

Not far from the Sakonnet River, on Rhode Island's eastern shore, this hike takes you through land that the Tiverton community fought hard to preserve. Wood roads and footpaths wind though mixed woodland, pastures long since abandoned and grown over, and a working farm that's alive and well.

Distance: 5.1-mile lollipop
Approximate hiking time: 2.5 hours
Difficulty: Moderate
Elevation gain: 105 feet
Trail surface: Wood road, forested path
Best season: Apr–Oct
Other trail users: Cross-country skiers, snowshoers, horseback riders

Canine compatibility: Dogs must be on leash at all times
Permits and fees: None
Schedule: Open year-round from sunrise to sunset
Maps: TOPO! New England; map on signboard near trailhead
Trail contact: Town of Tiverton Open Space Commission, 343 Highland Rd., Tiverton, RI 02878; (401) 625-6700; www.tiverton.ri .gov/boards/conservation.php

Finding the trailhead: From Route 24 in Tiverton, take Route 77 south for approximately 5 miles to a four-way intersection, which is Tiverton Four Corners. Turn left (east) onto Route 179, and the trailhead parking area is after the first house to your left (north). The entrance is marked with signage.

The Hike

From the parking lot, walk down a long flat dirt road toward a green metal gate. After walking around this gate, you'll pass a large trail map posted on a signboard covered by a small roof. Continue on a flat, sandy road through a grassy area flanked with a stone wall and a working farm immediately to your left (west). After passing another gate, a stone wall separates you from marshy woods to the right (east). As soon as you enter the woods—after about 0.2 mile—do not turn right (east) on the Orange Trail but continue straight onto the Yellow Trail—these trails are marked with colored blazes. This intersection has a seating area made of cedar covered with a roof.

The wood road (Yellow Trail) continues relatively straight and flat, straddling a maintained field on the right (east) and a fairly well-formed stone wall on the left, which fronts medium-growth swamp maples interspersed with some larger old-growth trees. The trail surface is now a gravel farm road rutted in places. Cross a brook and head into complete forest at 0.3 mile, surrounded by wooded swamp mostly populated with swamp maple. If you look closely, you'll see holly trees in the mix, as well as beech.

Turn right (east) sharply at 0.5 mile, continuing on the Yellow Trail. Here you'll be departing the wood road onto a footpath across a less marshy forest floor surrounded by a larger mix of midgrowth hickory, ash, birch, and maple. Pass a cellar hole to your left as the trail continues, well marked with small circular metal signs with a silver background and trim with a yellow arrow in the foreground.

At the 0.6-mile mark you will come to a five-way inter-section. Go right to stay on Yellow Trail; then about 50 feet later take the right fork onto the Red Trail. The trail surface can be wet depending on the season and has now transitioned back to a wood road through the same mix of trees, as well as mountain laurel groves and small beech farther into the interior on either side of the route.

You'll reach another fork at 0.9 mile, as well as a brook crossing with some well-formed old stone foundations indicating mill ruins to your left (west). After crossing the brook, turn left (northwest), continuing on the Red Trail and walking up a slight incline that appears to have been roughly cobbled with small stones long ago to prevent erosion and improve traction.

Turn left (north) at yet another fork at 1.0 mile, onto the Green Trail. Walk on the flat trail, with laurel groves interspersed throughout the trees. At 1.1 miles cross a brook running through a low-lying marshy area roughly spanned with wooden planks. Depending on the season, you may have to navigate some muddy patches.

After this crossing, the mountain laurel gets denser and taller, creating a type of laurel forest rising at least 8 feet on either side. A little later, the forest opens up so you can see into the distance through small and medium beech and swamp maple, rather than being hemmed in.

At 1.3 miles navigate a wet area using stones rather than planks or a bridge. The Green Trail ends at an intersection with the Yellow Trail at 1.4 miles. Continue straight on the Yellow Trail, which will curve right (north). The Yellow Trail also goes south here—your return trip. Rock outcroppings poke sporadically through the forest floor. You'll notice a short spur leading up a gradual smooth rock cliff called High Rock from which you can get a good overview of the woods below.

At 1.8 miles you'll pass the South Trail to your left. Continue following the Yellow Trail, which transitions back to a wider wood road. Progressing farther, you'll notice a stone wall to your left (west) with a large rock tumble covered with moss behind it. After passing this tumble, the trail surface is noticeably more elevated and drier, surrounded by forest that includes larger oaks. The grade remains mostly flat, but you are higher in elevation with a much wider open forest floor.

At 2.0 miles you'll reach a three-way intersection with the Ridge and Cemetery Trails (you'll return to this point on the Cemetery Trail). Continue straight on the Yellow Trail. Just when you thought you had escaped any presence of wooded marsh, you'll pass through a wide expanse of low-lying woods mostly populated with swamp maple, along with some young beech, oak, and black birch.

You'll emerge from the woods onto the disused Lafayette Road at 2.5 miles. Go left (west) along Lafayette Road. You'll see two tall radio towers to your right (north) in a field. Continue straight through a green metal gate; then pass a dirt parking area to your left (south) at 2.7 miles, which is the Ridge Trail trailhead.

Walk for approximately another tenth of a mile along what is now a paved road. Just as the road inclines, look toward your left (south) for a narrow passage cutting through dense roadside brush and briars. It's easy to miss if you're not paying attention, but you'll see a small (tiny, actually) white sign reading WELCOME TO THE PARDON GRAY PRESERVE. Follow this footpath—the Lafayette Connector—through swamp maples, some cherry trees, and increasingly dense under-growth populated with honeysuckle. The trail opens up into a wide-open working field at 2.9 miles.

Turn left (east) at the electric fence then right (south) at the field's corner to follow the wood line until you reach the 3.1-mile mark and a trail to your left (east) denoted by a small sign with a red marking and another with a black arrow on a white background. Take this trail to the left to reenter the woods and follow the red trail markers. This is the

Cemetery Trail. Even though the forest floor is initially wet, swamp maples increasingly yield to golden and black birch, oak, and holly trees. Soon the trail will begin to gradually climb. Homesites were planned for this land, but the Tiverton Land Trust saved 230 acres from that fate.

A split in the red marked Cemetery Trail at the 3.4-mile mark presents you with the choice of either bearing left (northeast) or veering off to the right (south). Bear left to stay on the Cemetery Trail.

At about 3.6 miles you'll encounter a four-way inter-section. Turn right (east). After approximately 50 feet you will reach the intersection with the Yellow Trail. Turn right (south) to follow the Yellow Trail back to the parking lot where you started.

The Yellow Trail transitions into a narrow footpath again, and holly will be part of the mix of trees on either side of the trail. A brook flows underneath the trail through a sluice at 4.1 miles, and the trail surface widens into a gravel and sand wood road once again. An unmarked wood road veers off to the right (east) through dense underbrush. Continue straight (south) on the Yellow Trail, past the Blue Trail intersection to your left (west), and once you pass the Red Trail to your left (west), you have completed the loop. Continue on the Yellow Trail back to the parking lot.

Miles and Directions

0.0   Begin at parking lot, toward a green metal gate.

0.2   Continue straight (north) at the fork, onto the Yellow Trail. Cross a brook into a wooded swamp.

0.5   Turn right (east) sharply, continuing on the Yellow Trail.

0.6   Turn right (east) at the fork onto the Red Trail.

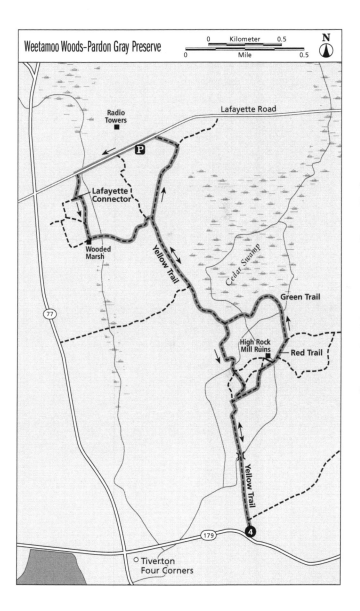

Weetamoo Woods–Pardon Gray Preserve

0   Kilometer   0.5
0   Mile   0.5

N

Lafayette Road

Radio Towers

P

Lafayette Connector

Wooded Marsh

Yellow Trail

Cedar Swamp

Green Trail

High Rock Mill Ruins

Red Trail

77

Yellow Trail

4

179

Tiverton Four Corners

0.9 Cross a brook and pass the old stone foundations and mill ruins.

1.0 Turn left (north) at the fork onto the Green Trail.

1.3 Parallel a brook before crossing it, then continue straight (north) onto the Yellow Trail at an intersection.

2.5 Turn left (west) after emerging onto the disused Lafayette Road.

2.8 Turn left (south) off Lafayette Road just as you reach an incline onto a footpath (Lafayette Connector).

2.9 Enter a wide-open working field. Turn left (east) at the electric fence; then turn right at the corner to follow the wood line.

3.1 Turn left (east) back into wooded marsh though brush.

3.4 Bear left (northeast) at a split in the Cemetery Trail.

3.6 Come to a four-way intersection and turn right (east); then about 50 feet later turn right (south) back on the Yellow Trail.

4.1 Cross a brook that flows underneath the trail through a sluice.

5.1 Arrive back at the trailhead.

5 Simmons Mill Pond

Entirely over sand, gravel, and grass, wide flat wood roads take you past several prime fishing ponds.

Distance: 2.3-mile lollipop
Approximate hiking time: 1.5 hours
Difficulty: Easy
Elevation gain: 68 feet
Trail surface: Wood roads
Best season: Apr–Oct
Other trail users: Cross-country skiers, snowshoers
Canine compatibility: Dogs must be on leash at all times

Permits and fees: None
Schedule: Open year-round from sunrise to sunset
Maps: TOPO! New England; map board near trailhead
Trail contact: State of Rhode Island DEM–Division of Parks & Recreation Headquarters, 1100 Tower Hill Rd., North Kingstown, RI 02852; (401) 667-6200; www .riparks.com

Finding the trailhead: From Tiverton Four Corners, take Route 179 south into Adamsville. Turn right (west) at the first intersection onto Cold Brook Road (immediately after passing a liquor store). Proceed up a steep hill, continuing for approximately 1.5 miles to the trailhead. A parking lot marked with signage is on the left (southeast).

The Hike

As you're standing in the dirt parking lot facing the trailhead behind a brown metal gate, take a moment to walk left and check out a small historical burial plot hidden in the grass. Additionally, throughout this hike there are many historical markers—often on book-sized pieces of wood—replete with old photographs, images, and text.

This hike is also an excellent place to bring your fishing rod since you're passing three ponds in close proximity that have signs indicating that they are trout waters.

Once you walk around the gate, you'll be on a wide sand and gravel access road that appears to be regularly used by vehicles. A map board covered with a small roof is up ahead to your right. The grade is flat at the beginning, followed by a slight but steady decline surrounded by small- to mid-growth oak, swamp maple, beech, laurel, and prominent well-established holly trees. You'll notice some unmarked wood roads branching off to the right (southwest), but continue straight (southeast) on the main road down toward Simmons Mill Pond.

Soon you'll be able to see water through the trees and at 0.5 mile, cross the dam. From here you'll get a good view of the pond's entire length.

Bear right (southeast) at a fork just past the dam on a wide wood road where the surface transitions from sandy gravel to mostly grass. Moving away from the pond shore on a relatively flat grade, 0.8 mile marks another split. Continue to the left (southeast), where you'll cross another dam with a spillway that helps contain a small pond. You have a choice of continuing on a grassy access road at the base of the dam or climbing up onto the dam itself. Both options lead in the same direction, but make sure you merge onto the wood road that hugs the pond shore close to your left (northwest) after passing the dam.

The trail skirts this pond's edge to the 1.0-mile mark, where you'll cross a spillway made of concrete topped with a narrow walkway fitted with metal railings. From here, continue straight ahead following the wood road away from the pond.

The trail veers into the woods and at 1.1 miles reaches an intersection with the John Dyer Road parking lot spur. Bear left to follow the main trail, which at 1.2 miles passes through a stone wall. The trail becomes a wide-open grassy access road lined with well-formed stone walls on either side. Since it's so straight and unobstructed, you can see at least a half mile ahead into the distance.

At about the 1.3-mile mark you'll reach an intersection. For this hike go left (west), but you can continue either straight ahead or to the right to add another loop, thereby turning the hike into a figure eight. Then at 1.5 miles pass over an earthen and stone dam that overflows in wet weather.

Upon reaching the site of what was once a red cabin fronted by a deck overlooking the water at about 1.6 miles—there is a marker with old photos of the cabin—you'll get another view of Simmons Mill Pond to your right (west). Continuing on the access road with the pond to your right, complete the loop by crossing over the Simmons Mill Pond dam and retracing your steps back to the parking lot.

Miles and Directions

0.0   Begin by walking behind a brown metal gate.

0.5   Cross Simmons Mill Pond dam.

0.8   Move away from the pond shore on a relatively flat grade; then cross another dam with a spillway.

1.0   Cross a concrete spillway; then continue straight on the main trail into the woods.

1.1   Bear left (west) past the John Dyer Road lot spur.

1.2   Pass through a stone wall and continue on the main trail lined with stone walls.

1.3   Turn left at the intersection, though you can add another loop by continuing straight (north) or going right (east).

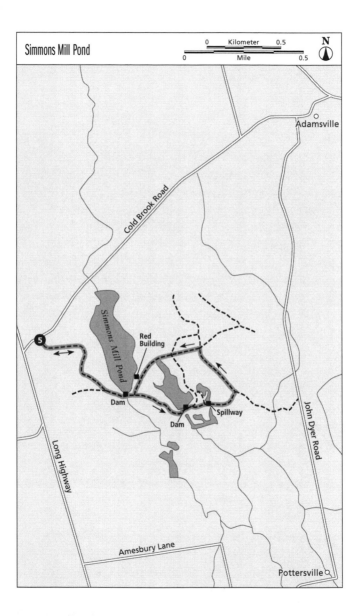

1.5 Pass over an earthen and stone dam.

1.6 Pass the site of what was once a red cabin overlooking Simmons Mill Pond. Soon after, you will close the loop by returning to the main trail you walked in on.

2.3 Arrive back at the trailhead.

6 Carbuncle Pond–Moosup River

This hike passes through impressive pine groves, wooded marsh, and several wide-open and extensive fields. You'll skirt a diverse mix of landscapes, but one consistent feature throughout is human usage, readily apparent via tire tracks on many trail beds, abandoned sandpits, and remnants of agricultural lands marked with stone walls fringing large swaths of meadow.

Distance: 2.7-mile lollipop
Approximate hiking time: 2 hours
Difficulty: Easy
Elevation gain: 79 feet
Trail surface: Wood roads, footpaths
Best season: Apr–Oct
Other trail users: Cross-country skiers, snowshoers, horseback riders, ATVs

Canine compatibility: Dogs must be on leash at all times
Permits and fees: None
Schedule: Open year-round sunrise to sunset
Maps: TOPO! New England
Trail contact: State of Rhode Island DEM–Division of Parks & Recreation Headquarters, 1100 Tower Hill Rd., North Kingstown, RI 02852; (401) 667-6200; www.riparks.com

Finding the trailhead: The trailhead is off Route 14 heading west from Providence, near the Connecticut state line. Look for the CARBUNCLE POND FISHING AREA sign, which is approximately 1 mile west of the junction with Route 117, on your left (south). From the west, traveling from the Connecticut border, it's approximately 1.5 miles on your right. Follow a dirt road down to the first parking lot, where you'll see a wooden fishing dock extending out into the water to your right (west).

The Hike

Walk down the dirt road from the first parking lot, surrounded by red pine groves, through a second parking lot with a boat launch then through a set of large rocks at the end of the lot onto the trail. Continue following the sandy pond shore with water views immediately to your right (west) until you reach what was once a beach area and small parking area marked with a metal guardrail. It's now closed off to swimming, and the sand parking lot is overgrown with weeds.

With the guardrail to your right, turn left (southwest) at about the 0.3-mile mark at the back of an open sandy area onto an access road that straddles a dense mix of pine and oak to your left (east) and an extensive marsh immediately to your right (west). The trail's sandy surface and relatively flat terrain has made it popular with ATVs. Worn tire tracks are readily apparent in this section.

Pass through a four-way intersection at about 0.4 mile and continue straight on the main road to about the 0.5-mile mark, where you'll depart from marsh views into dense red pine groves on either side. Make your first small and short climb, winding through the trees up to a T intersection at 0.6 mile at an abandoned rail bed, now a wide dirt road. You can see a long distance in either direction due to the fact that the rail bed is straight and flat. Turn left (east), and after a few steps, make another sharp left (north) turn onto the blue-blazed trail, which is clearly marked on a medium-size red pine.

Head into dense red pine again, treading along a sandy trail surface. Even though signs of heavy ATV usage continue to be prevalent, the surroundings are scenic, with an open forest floor populated with a mix of new- and medium-growth red pine, large white pine, and small oak saplings. It's almost impossible to stray from the route, which continues to be a wide wood road, well marked with prominent blue markings.

You'll reach an intersection at 1.0 mile with a smaller trail branching down into the woods to your right (east). Ignore the trail that departs to the left and look ahead for a post with a blue blaze on it. Straight ahead you'll see a small open field. Continue on the path through the field and then down a small hill. At the bottom, turn right (east) at a white post with a blue square (about 1.1 miles) marking the Blue Trail intersection. Wind down a steep embankment through dense pine on a narrow footpath into a grassy clearing; then follow the dirt road right toward a small waterfall on the Moosup River. The falls are visible coursing over solid rock. The waterfall itself isn't huge but gradually cascades over a massive rock outcropping.

At about 1.2 miles, continue straight (north) past the waterfall, ignoring the trail that departs up the bank to the left (also marked with blue blazes, though these are circular), to continue on the Blue Trail (a.k.a. the National Scenic Trail [NST]). You'll parallel the river, with the water close by to your right. The trail narrows into a footpath for the first time. You'll see a dense pine grove up an embankment to your left and several heavily used fishing spots along the water's edge as you progress.

Climb a small, steep ridge at 1.3 miles—bearing right to parallel the river—where you overlook the river and the wide-open pine forest. The contrast makes a pretty scene. This segment is well marked with blue blazes. After skirting the pine grove, head back down into a low-lying wooded area next to the river. Thick brush separates you from the water, blocking visibility. Soon you'll exit this brush into a grassy field. Continue following the blue blazes along the field's edge into a dense white pine grove. Farther on you'll see some large pines that appear to be close to one hundred years old.

Turn right (east) onto a well-established wood road at about 1.5 miles and head down toward a wide-open field. Upon entering the field, follow the herd path across the field (BE CAREFUL OF TICKS) toward a post with a blue marker on it that may be obscured. However, as you progress toward the field's left corner, you'll see a large pine grove, and soon the post will be visible through tall grasses and underbrush if it's spring or summer.

After passing this blue-marked post, you'll enter a massive pine grove. The trail continues on a slight incline, but overall, the walking is easy. You'll pass a great vantage point within the pines at 1.5 miles, offering elevated 360-degree views of these stately trees.

Another crucial intersection is at about the 1.9-mile mark, where you'll see a field through the trees to your left (west). The Blue Trail continues straight ahead (north) out to Route 14. Turn left (west) into the field via a short access trail, and then parallel the woods line on the field's left edge. To your right, the field extends to Route 14, which is now visible, and up ahead you'll see a brown signboard at the top of the hill you are climbing.

Soon you'll reach a dirt access road leading from Route 14 through a brown metal gate up to where you are now standing. Follow this sand and gravel road away from Route 14 through the longest expanse of field on the entire route. Mixed forest surrounds the field on either side. You'll enter

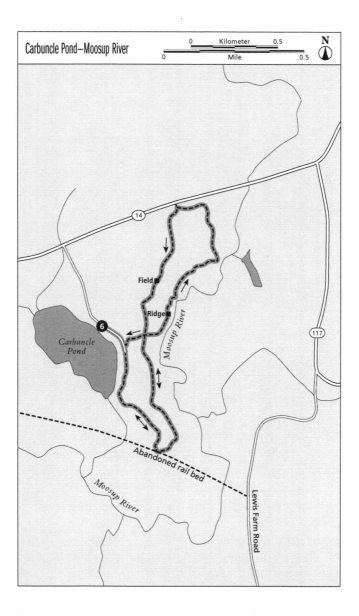

N

0   Kilometer   0.5

0   Mile   0.5

14

Field

Ridge

6

Carbuncle
Pond

Moosup River

Abandoned rail bed

Moosup River

117

Lewis Farm Road

woods for a brief period at 2.1 miles before emerging into another sandy field populated with a mix of trees. After passing this field, walk straight through a sandy intersection at about 2.3 miles on a flat access road, completing the loop when you reach the white post with blue marker (about 2.5 miles) you encountered earlier.

From here, turn right (west) and follow the wood road back to the boat launch parking lot.

Miles and Directions

0.0 Walk down dirt road from first parking lot.

0.5 Continue straight into dense red pine groves; then climb to a T intersection at an abandoned rail bed. Turn left (east), then left again (north) on the blue-blazed trail.

1.0 Continue straight at an intersection down toward a small open field. Follow the path down to the waterfall on the Moosup River.

1.3 Climb a steep ridge overlooking the river.

1.9 Turn left (west) on a small access trail leading to a large field flowing uphill toward a brown signboard at its top.

2.1 Enter woods for a brief period before emerging into another sandy field.

2.3 Walk straight through a sandy intersection at the edge of the field on a flat access road.

2.5 Close the loop at the white post with the blue mark you passed earlier. Turn right (west) to head back to parking lot.

2.7 Arrive back at the trailhead.

7 George B. Parker Woodland

This route passes through an Audubon Society nature preserve containing some interesting historical relics and unique
natural features. Highlights include stone cairns, a wooded
lane from the American Revolution, perfectly formed stone
foundations, and striking rock outcroppings.

Distance: 3.3-mile lollipop
Approximate hiking time: 3.5
hours includes time to explore
historical sites
Difficulty: Moderate
Elevation gain: 248 feet
Trail surface: Wood roads,
footpaths
Best season: Apr–Oct
Other trail users: Snowshoers
Canine compatibility: No dogs
permitted

Permits and fees: None
Schedule: Open year-round from
sunrise to sunset
Maps: TOPO! New England;
www.asri.org/refuges/george
-b.-parker-woodland.html; map
board at trailhead
Trail contact: Audubon Society
of Rhode Island; 12 Sanderson
Rd., Smithfield, RI 02917; (401)
949-5454; www.asri.org/refuges/
george-b.-parker-woodland.html

Finding the trailhead: From Route 102 west of Providence, travel
south of RI 14 and turn left (east) onto Maple Valley Road. Or, traveling north on Route 102, pass RI 117 and turn right (east) onto Maple
Valley Road. The parking lot is immediately after the first house to
the north. A brown wooden gate and sign mark the dirt parking lot
entrance.

The Hike

The trail begins alongside a map board at the back of the
parking lot. Begin on the Orange Trail at the head of the

parking lot, going north. You'll quickly reach a T intersection with a signpost indicating that the Meadow Trail is to your left (west) and the Forest Trail is to your right (east). Turn right, continuing down a footpath through cedar mixed with pine that becomes mostly deciduous swamp maple, birch, and undergrowth. The trail is well marked, and you'll parallel a stone wall to the right before curving away from it and continuing to wind down through the woods.

Follow a signpost pointing left for the Orange Trail to Blue Trail and climb down some wooden steps, passing through wooded swamp. At about 0.2 mile you'll begin crossing a series of wooden planks over this terrain. The planks transition into an extensive wooden walkway with railings on either side, eventually crossing a slow-moving stream.

Upon reaching an intersection at 0.5 mile, turn left (west) onto the Blue Trail, and make a quick scramble over some rocks. Right after this intersection the trail navigates through boulders surrounded by medium-growth swamp maples and birches. Enough open space between the trees has allowed grasses to carpet the forest floor in spots. Some small climbs wind over portions of rock ledge at a gradual grade.

You'll notice that the mix of trees on either side is ever changing.

At 1.0 mile, you'll cross Biscuit Hill Road, a wide and level wood road lined by two parallel stone walls. Pass through a well-crafted threshold through the far (second) stone wall, and you'll immediately come to the stone foundation of the Vaughn Farm site recessed into the ground to your left (north). It's surprisingly well formed, with stone steps still solidly intact leading into what once was the cellar.

After passing these historical remnants, you'll quickly enter a woodland of mostly pine mixed with beech and oak.

Head down through a stone wall into a mixed forest of pine and medium-growth oak. At 1.1 miles, pass around the end of yet another stone wall; then at 1.2 miles you'll make a slight climb onto a plateau within the woods surrounded by mostly midgrowth oak. A ridgeline poking up from the forest floor is visible in the woods to your left.

Wind down through these rocky outcroppings and pass through low-lying wild blueberry bushes. You'll have some wooded views as you continue the gradual descent. Climb down past an interesting rock outcropping immediately to your left (north), punctuated by a pointed stone and a small cave recessed into the ledge. Continue through midgrowth oaks as you wind downward to the intersection of an unmarked trail—possibly a defunct wood road—at about 1.4 miles. Continue straight (south) on the Blue Trail.

After winding past two large boulders, the trail levels out for a stretch, through mostly oak, before descending again through some more large moss-covered boulders. Soon you'll reach flatter terrain at about 1.6 miles, paralleling a brook to your left for a few steps, before beginning a steady climb. At 1.7 miles you'll end this gradual but steady climbing as the trail levels out. Also, be sure to bear right at the intersection of an unmarked trail near the 1.7-mile mark. Stay left at another unmarked trail at 1.8 miles.

You can't miss the spot, marked with a gigantic boulder, where the Yellow Trail crosses the Blue at about 1.9 miles. Continue straight on Blue.

After this intersection, you'll begin to hear a stream in the distance, and then you'll see Pine Swamp Brook through the trees to your left (east). Cross Biscuit Hill Road again just beyond the 2.2-mile mark, continuing to follow the Blue Trail. You'll hear cascading water in the distance.

Soon the trail climbs up above the streambed, putting you almost vertically over the water. As you continue climbing along the ridge above this swiftly moving stream, you'll pass a medium-size beech tree that has been heavily inscribed with initials over the years. The 2.4-mile mark features a clear bird's-eye view of the stream directly below from a relatively high elevation. You'll be separated by some underbrush and trees but still have good visibility.

From here, you'll descend to the streambed, a radical departure from where you were just a few minutes before. At 2.5 miles cross over the Yellow Trail, continuing on the Blue, and as you do so, you'll notice that down to your left (south), a wooden footbridge spans the stream leading to parking lot #2.

You'll begin passing clusters of stone cairns on either side of the trail in the woods at 2.6 miles. Some are still well formed while others have crumbled to the forest floor. Adding to the mystique of these structures, some are built into a hillside that you'll be winding up, giving their placement no apparent strategic purpose. Boundary or grave markers seem highly unlikely.

Continue higher up into the woods, passing a big flat stone ridgetop covered with a large patch of grass to your right. Shortly after passing this, you'll complete the loop by intersecting the Orange Trail at 2.9 miles.

Turn left (south) onto the Orange Trail and retrace your steps back up to the parking lot.

Miles and Directions

0.0   Begin on the Orange Trail.

0.2   Cross a series of wooden planks leading to a walkway and bridge.

George B. Parker Woodland

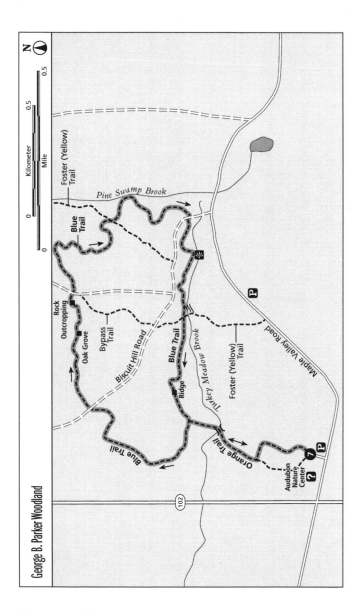

0.5 Turn left (north)[AU: Above text says left (west); please reconcile] onto the Blue Trail.

1.0 Cross Biscuit Hill Road; then pass the Vaughn Farm foundation and stone walls.

1.2 Climb up onto a plateau in the woods; then wind down through rocky outcroppings.

1.4 Continue straight through a wood road intersection on the Blue Trail.

1.7 End a long, gradual climb. Stay right at an unmarked trail that goes to the left. Soon after, bear right past another intersection with an unmarked trail.

1.9 Continue east on Blue Trail at an intersection with the Yellow Trail marked with a gigantic boulder.

2.2 Cross Biscuit Hill Road again, continuing on the Blue Trail.

2.4 Enjoy a bird's-eye view of the stream below.

2.6 Begin passing stone cairn clusters on either side of the trail.

2.9 Close the loop and return back to parking lot via Orange Trail.

3.3 Arrive back at the trailhead.

8 Barden Reservoir

Scenic views on this route really come into prominence as soon as you head east on Hemlock Road and pass some extensive red pine groves. Midway into the hike, you'll be treated to some full reservoir views and then get to explore a massive stone spillway. Complete the loop by walking along a country lane past a historical cemetery and a farmstead then heading back out to Central Pike.

Distance: 4.5-mile loop
Approximate hiking time: 2 hours
Difficulty: Easy
Elevation gain: 176 feet
Trail surface: Paved and dirt roads
Best season: Apr–Oct
Other trail users: Horseback riders and cars

Canine compatibility: Dogs must be on leash at all times
Permits and fees: None
Schedule: Open year-round sunrise to sunset
Maps: TOPO! New England
Trail contact: Town of Foster, 181 Howard Hill Rd., Foster, RI 02825; (401) 392-9200

Finding the trailhead: From Route 102 west of Providence and just south of US 6, head west on Central Pike (northbound turn left; southbound turn right). After approximately 1.6 miles, immediately upon crossing a bridge over a portion of the reservoir, park on either side of the Central Pike in sandy turnouts. A historical cemetery is up on a hill to your left (south).

The Hike

From the parking areas, walk along the Central Pike to the west. At your first left, turn south onto Kate Randall Road, which quickly transitions to dirt. A red pine grove to the left (east) separates you from the reservoir in the distance. A brook crosses underneath the trail through a stone sluice at 0.3 mile. You'll be traveling through mostly deciduous forest, with some pines mixed in with oak, swamp maple, and hickory.

At 0.7 mile pass the first house, on the right side of this mostly residential road that's lightly populated. Pass your first stately grove of red pine close to your left (east), fronted by a stone wall, at 0.9 mile, and then reach an intersection with Hemlock Road to your left (east) and Mill Road to your right (west). Turn left onto Hemlock Road, a dirt road, traveling down a slight and steady grade past houses mostly to your left (north) within mixed woods of oak, beech, and pine.

Pass a red pine grove close to the road extending into the forest to your left at 1.2 miles. Here, the road also noticeably straightens out and begins to pass through increasingly dense pine forest on either side, with any kind of residential presence all but disappearing. You are definitely surrounded by more rugged terrain. At 1.4 miles, pass around a gate marking the end of the paved, open road to walk on a wood road. This is where it truly gets scenic while offering the benefit of walking along a well-graded dirt road.

After crossing a bridge just large enough for one car at 1.8 miles, you'll have close-up views of the reservoir to your left (north) and a marsh to your right (south). You'll pass into a more mixed forest with fewer pine, and reservoir views continue through the trees as you parallel the shore.

Hemlock Road transitions back to pavement, and at 2.3 miles you'll pass a spillway to your left (north). Here you can take a small footpath through the trees to explore. A little beyond the spillway, you'll reach a T intersection where you'll turn left (northwest) onto Ponagansett Road, crossing the spillway stream. After the crossing, the road transitions back to a dirt surface and you'll be surrounded by undergrowth and meadow grasses. You'll also pass a beautiful and well-kept historical Barden Cemetery to your right (east), surrounded by almost perfectly formed walls built with large blocks of stone.

As you continue, fairly clear water views to your left (west) will be readily apparent. The woods surrounding the road are almost 100 percent deciduous. You'll begin a moderate climb at 2.9 miles, with loose stone walls tumbling down the embankments on either side of the road. As you move away from the clear water views, smaller oak trees and an embankment separate you from the water. After a moderate climb, at the top of the hill at about 3.4 miles, Holdsworth Farm to your right (east) appears to have been on this plot for centuries.

Pass a field to your right (west) at 3.8 miles, and then you'll reach the T intersection with Central Pike at about 4.0 miles. Turn left (west) here and walk down a long hill, crossing the bridge back to your car.

Miles and Directions

0.0 Go west from the parking areas to a left (south) turn onto Kate Randall Road.

0.3 Cross a brook running through a stone sluice underneath the road.

0.7 Pass the first house to the right (west).

0.9 Pass a red pine grove; then turn left (east) onto Hemlock Road.

1.2 Pass a red pine grove close to the road.

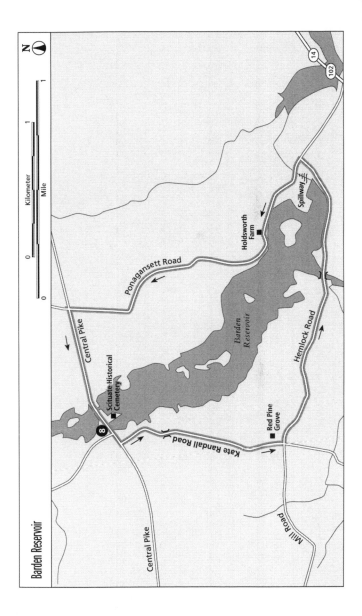

Barden Reservoir

1.4 Pass around a gate where the paved road transitions to a wood road.

1.8 Cross a bridge only wide enough for one car to pass.

2.3 Pass a spillway to your left (north). Turn left (northwest) on Ponagansett Road.

2.9 Begin a moderate climb.

3.4 Pass Holdsworth Farm.

3.8 Pass a field to your right.

4.0 Upon reaching a T intersection with Central Pike, turn left (west) and walk down a long hill.

4.5 Arrive back at your car.

9 Blackstone Gorge

Even though it's a short walk, this route is the only one in Rhode Island, within the entire Blackstone Valley, that puts you high above the river gorge with sweeping views of the tumultuous waters coursing through a near-vertical stone canyon.

Distance: 0.8 mile out and back
Approximate hiking time: 1 hour
Difficulty: Easy
Elevation gain: 47 feet
Trail surface: Footpaths surfaced with stone dust and dirt
Best season: Apr–Oct
Other trail users: Snowshoers
Canine compatibility: Dogs must be on leash at all times
Permits and fees: None

Schedule: Open year-round from sunrise to sunset
Maps: TOPO! New England; www.mass.gov/dcr/parks/trails/print/BlackstoneMap.pdf
Trail contact: Department of Conservation and Recreation, 251 Causeway St., Suite 600, Boston, MA; (617) 626-1250, mass.parks@state.ma.us

Finding the trailhead: From Providence, take Route 122 north to the border town of Blackstone, Massachusetts. As soon as you cross a bridge, you will see a town green to your left (south). Turn left (south) at this green onto Butler Street, and then take your next right (west) turn onto County Street. Drive to the end of this street, and parking lot will be to your left (south). Falls are visible straight ahead.

The Hike

Begin on a stone-dust trail leading away from the parking lot down to the spillway. The trail is clearly marked with signage, and you'll see the falls and a boat launch ramp above the dam ahead through the trees. After checking out the cascading water close up, continue on a stone-dust trail leading down to the left (south), passing a black wrought iron fence to your right.

The trail parallels the river gorge to your right (west) and winds through a mix of mountain laurel, small hemlock, and oak on a relatively flat surface punctuated with rocks poking out of the forest floor. There are plenty of opportunities to get close-up water views via side trails leading to cliffs overhanging the gorge.

You'll see numerous herd paths winding around each other, some traveling off to the left away from the water. For this hike, the water is the primary visual element so be sure to follow the trail that follows the contour of the river.

Bear right (east) at an intersection at 0.1 mile, where you'll see a fire pit, and soon the trail surface transitions to rock. High up above the gorge, you'll have reasonably good views of the water through the hemlocks and consistently hear the rapids rushing below. Even though you'll be noticeably gaining elevation, the climb is gradual along the rock ridge.

The first in a series of spectacular overlooks begins at about 0.3 mile, with views straight down to the water as well as across to trees and jagged cliffs on the opposite shore. From here turn left, away from the gorge, into dense laurel, still on a rocky trail surface. Pass another overlook, accessible down through the trees to your right. Even though there are several paths paralleling the main route that can be explored, continue straight and soon you'll notice that the river appears to be still even though a swift undercurrent is present.

Enter a wide-open grassy area shaded with oaks that looks as though it used to be a picnic area. Here, the river's

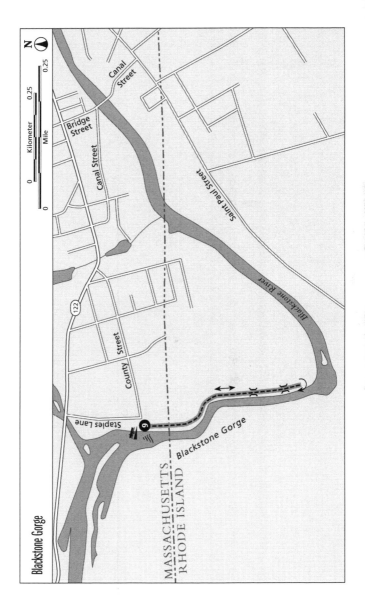

Blackstone Gorge

N

0   0.25
Kilometer
0   0.25
Mile

Canal Street

Bridge Street

Canal Street

122

County Street

Staples Lane

Saint Paul Street

Blackstone River

Blackstone Gorge

MASSACHUSETTS
RHODE ISLAND

9

edge is almost completely level with the ground, a big difference from just a few minutes before. Turn around here and retrace your steps back to the parking lot.

Miles and Directions

0.0 Begin on a stone-dust trail leading away from the parking lot down to the spillway.

0.1 Turn right (east) at an intersection where you'll see a fire pit.

0.3 Pass the first in a series of spectacular overlooks. Farther on another overlook is accessible down through the trees to your right.

0.4 Reach the river. Retrace your route back to the trailhead.

0.8 Arrive back at your car.

10 Buck Hill Management Area

This route passes through a vast expanse of deciduous woodland, large meadows, and wide swaths of clear-cut forest. Some fields contain crops like corn and grasses to attract wildlife. If you want to get away from it all and possibly not see another human for hours, this is your destination.

Distance: 3.5-mile loop
Approximate hiking time: 2.5 hours
Difficulty: Easy
Elevation gain: 108 feet
Trail surface: Wood roads, footpaths
Best season: Apr–Oct
Other trail users: Cross-country skiers, snowshoers
Canine compatibility: Dogs must be on leash at all times

Permits and fees: None
Schedule: Open year-round from sunrise to sunset
Maps: TOPO! New England; map available at trailhead
Trail contact: State of Rhode Island DEM—Division of Parks & Recreation Headquarters, 1100 Tower Hill Rd., North Kingstown, RI 02852; (401) 667-6200; www .riparks.com

Finding the trailhead: Located in the northwest corner of Rhode Island near the Connecticut state line, it's easy to miss the parking lot for this trailhead. The easiest method is to set your odometer at soon as you turn west onto Buck Hill Road from the intersection of Route 100 coming from either the north or south. When the odometer reads 2.2 miles, you have reached the parking lot entrance to your right (north). Drive uphill on a gravel road to a large sandy parking lot.

The Hike

The trail begins behind a brown metal gate that's readily apparent at the far end of the lot. Continue on a flat dirt road through a field, and to your right (east) you'll see a brown signboard affixed with a trail map.

The road bears off to the right through deciduous forest. Cross through a pine grove and turn right (northeast) at an intersection at about 0.2 mile. Here you'll see what appears to be a square foundation sunken into the ground to your right with a small stream filling it and running through it. Since it's so small and close to the trail's edge, it may have been a watering hole.

The wood road continues through small beech, swamp maple, and oak. To your left (west), a little past the foundation, you'll see another wood road leading up to a clearing overlooking a marsh. Continue on the main trail, paralleling this marsh through the trees to your left.

A little farther along, other side trails to the left (west) provide more opportunities to get clearer marsh views. Continue left (north) at a fork in the trail upon reaching 0.4 mile, following the Yellow Trail with its prominent yellow trail markings. Pass a dense hemlock forest to your right (east), and up ahead you'll see the marsh coming into view as you pass through an open grassy area. The trail climbs over an earthen berm before it transitions back into a narrow footpath entering the forest once more. Evergreens are on either side, and the terrain becomes more rugged.

You'll continue to see yellow markings, and even though the trail is more rugged, it's still relatively flat. You're walking on a stony surface with the marsh close to your left (west), separated by dense underbrush. After passing through hemlock, you'll enter a mix of deciduous trees. The trail bed is still rocky but wider, giving it the appearance of a winding wagon road paved with rock and passing through midgrowth oak and beech. Two features are certain along this stretch:

you have moved away from the marsh and the trail continues to be well marked with yellow. The trail surface resembles a dried-up streambed filled with rocks. The canopy above allows plenty of sunshine through, which encourages the growth of numerous deciduous saplings.

At the 0.9-mile mark, reach another intersection where a fire road crosses the trail, but continue on the rock-strewn Yellow Trail. As you continue, you'll encounter more rocks and ruts surrounded by loads of ground-level wild blueberries, making this area a treat if you're hiking during July.

The trail bed becomes noticeably less rocky at 1.2 miles, transitioning away from the "streambed effect" into a mostly dirt surface. Cross through a stone wall and pass a cellar hole close to your left (west), and then begin a slight but steady decline that is noticeable since this is the first occurrence on the route so far. Laurel also becomes more prominent in the mix of vegetation surrounding you on the low-lying forest floor, which is crisscrossed with stone walls.

Turn left (west) onto Old Starr Road, another well-formed wood road strewn with medium-size boulders, at 1.5 miles. Continue on a gradual decline though mixed deciduous and evergreen trees. At the bottom of this gradual hill, the trail opens out into a grassy area surrounded by marsh. Pines will be in the mix of trees to your right (north), and the trail surface is no longer stony but covered with grass.

Leave Old Starr Road at 1.7 miles by forking off to the left (southwest) onto Benson Mountain Trail, a noticeably well-traveled wood road due to exposed sand and ruts. The grassy wood road now opens up considerably and is wide enough for two vehicles to pass side by side. To your right (west), through the trees, you'll see a marshy pond with a waterfowl box posted above the water. After making a gradual climb, the trail levels out and remains wide and grassy, interspersed with wildflowers depending on the season, giving it the appearance of a narrow alpine meadow snaking through the forest.

At about 2.2 miles, to your right (west) you'll see dense pine, and to the left and right, through the trees, you'll see fields that will figure more prominently with access roads on either side leading to them. It looks as if the grasses have been planted in them for wildlife habitat.

After passing dense pines to your left (east), a field becomes visible through the trees. The trail then widens back out into a narrow strip of alpine meadow. Dense pine groves continue to your left (west), and you'll see open and recovering clear-cuts through the trees.

At about 2.4 miles the logged area squarely meets the trail's left edge.

Depart from the wide grassy trail at 3.0 miles, bearing left (south) to follow the road. During summer, you may hear cars racing in the distance at nearby Thompson Motor Speedway.

The trail becomes curvier as it winds downhill toward the access road you came in on. Complete the loop by turning right (south) at the access road intersection and retrace your steps back to the parking lot.

Miles and Directions

0.0 Begin behind a brown metal gate.

0.2 Cross through a pine grove; then turn right (northeast) at an intersection.

0.4 Continue left at a fork in the trail, following prominent yellow markings.

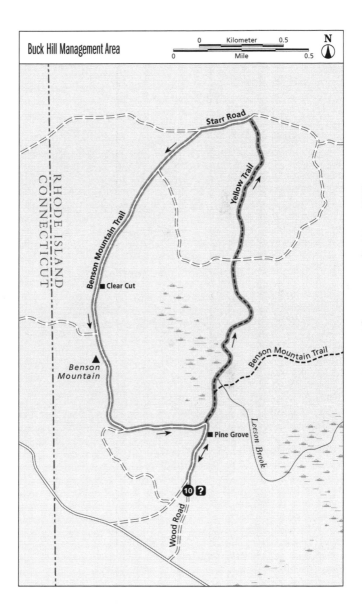

0   Kilometer   0.5

0   Mile   0.5

N

RHODE ISLAND
CONNECTICUT

Starr Road

Yellow Trail

Benson Mountain Trail

■ Clear Cut

▲ Benson Mountain

Benson Mountain Trail

Leeson Brook

■ Pine Grove

10 ?

Wood Road

0.9 Continue on the rock-strewn Yellow Trail at its intersection with a fire road.

1.2 The trail bed becomes less rocky, transitioning a mostly dirt surface.

1.5 Turn left (west) onto Old Starr Road.

1.7 Bear left (southwest) at T intersection, continuing on the well-traveled Benson Mountain Trail.

2.2 The trail passes through a mix of dense pines and open and recovering clear-cuts.

2.4 A recovering logged area meets the trail's left edge.

3.0 Depart from the meadow trail, turning left (south) onto a wood road.

3.5 Arrive back at your car.

11 Durfee Hill Management Area

This route passes through extensive pine forest, wide-open fields, marshland, and around a pond.

Distance: 3.1-mile loop
Approximate hiking time: 2 hours 15 minutes
Difficulty: Moderate due to length; follow directions here carefully—the trails are not marked!
Elevation gain: 107 feet
Trail surface: Wood roads, footpaths
Best season: Apr–Oct
Other trail users: Cross-country skiers, snowshoers, ATVs

Canine compatibility: Dogs must be on leash at all times
Permits and fees: None
Schedule: Open year-round from sunrise to sunset
Maps: TOPO! New England; map (or map board) at trailhead
Trail contact: State of Rhode Island DEM—Division of Parks & Recreation Headquarters, 1100 Tower Hill Rd., North Kingstown, RI 02852; (401) 667-6200; www .riparks.com

Finding the trailhead: This hike is located several miles from the Connecticut border in the northwest portion of Rhode Island. From US 44 take Route 94 south. As soon as you make this turn, set your odometer and go 1.3 miles. A reddish-brown sign with yellow lettering to your left (east) marks the parking lot entrance off Route 94.

The Hike

The sand parking lot is high on a hill overlooking a marsh and a pond off to the left (southeast). To reach the trailhead, walk back out of the parking lot entrance and turn left (southwest) onto Route 94, walking down a hill. Just before utility pole 33½ at 0.2 mile, you will find the unmarked and narrow trailhead to your right (west), leading from the roadside after a set of metal guardrails. The trail is barely visible through a dense pine grove, but upon further inspection and once you progress inward, you'll notice that even though crowded in with saplings, this wide footpath parallels a large and imposing rock wall towering above the forest floor to your right (north). Some large portions of this cliff have tumbled down due to erosion. You'll be walking on a completely flat surface. As you progress, the outcropping consistently diminishes in size and height.

You'll reach a four-way intersection at 0.4 mile, where a footpath crosses the wood road. To your right (north), the footpath leads over what remains of the rock outcropping up a hill, and to your left (south) curves down a hill. Turn left (south), and soon you'll be heading down a rutted embankment carved out by mountain bikes and dirt bikes. Exposed stones jut out of the trail bed. Pass through mostly oak and some pine, and another rock outcropping appears though the trees to your right.

After making this descent, you'll reach another intersection at 0.5 mile. Turn right (west) onto a disused and rutted wood road enclosed by stately pine and hemlock. Soon you'll be climbing a small but steep hill, now surrounded by mostly pine to your left, along with oak and beech to your right.

After making this slight climb, the trail levels out under medium-growth pine forest. Red pine will be most prominent to your left, while the deciduous mix continues to your right. Once the trail curves sharply to the left (southwest), you will parallel the marsh—located down below to your right (west)—while walking through red pine forest that lushly carpets the trail bed with needles.

Reach another intersection at 0.8 miles, in a clearing overlooking a marsh that is now completely unobstructed. bear left (south), back into a rugged pine forest and away from the marsh, avoiding a footpath over a grass-covered berm that appears to act as a dam.

As you proceed on a flat grade, the trail bed is noticeably rutted due to ATV traffic, but the extensive pine forest surrounding you provides some picturesque views. At 1.0 mile, curve to the left (east) at a Y intersection.

The trail bed continues to be noticeably rutted by ATV and mountain bike activity. And soon, down through the trees to your right (south), you'll see a marsh. The trail makes a short, steep descent into a low-lying swampy area next to this marsh, barely visible through dense underbrush. After navigating over what can be an extremely muddy section depending on the season, continue on the footpath with the marsh close to the right.

After rounding the curve, turn left (south) at 1.2 miles. There are several herd paths and one that makes it seem like the trail continues straight to round a hillside. Instead, follow the trail (really, set of herd paths) left (southeast) up a brief but very steep climb studded with large pines toward a ridge. There's plenty of evidence of heavy ATV usage as portions of this hillside show signs of extreme erosion.

Upon reaching the top, you'll be rewarded with good, wooded views from a plateau high up on a ridge carpeted with pine needles. Continue following the trail to the left (northeast); then at about 1.3 miles turn right (south) at a T intersection onto another rutted footpath. Then at about 1.4 miles bear left (southeast) at a Y intersection.

Shortly before exiting the woods, you'll see and hear a stream cascading over rocks in a ravine down to your right (south), and at 1.5 miles you'll reach a three-way road inter-section, with the brook to your right in a small meadow. Turn left (northeast), walking up alongside Route 94, making a gradual but steady climb. Once the road levels out, you'll see a guardrail and an orange metal gate to your right (east). Turn right (east) here, at 1.7 miles, crossing the road and continu-ing behind the gate into pine forest, gradually curving to the right (southeast). As you round this corner, you'll see a historical cemetery for the town of Glocester up on a hill in the woods to your left (north).

After passing the cemetery, continue on the wood road; then turn left (northeast) at the next intersection. Immedi-ately surrounding the trail, densely packed small pine saplings vie for precious sunlight. The wood road ends at 1.8 miles in a sandy clearing that looks like it might have once been a sandpit. Continue across this clearing, up and over an earthen bank and left (east) down through a narrow passage through pine forest to a grassy wood road. Turn left (northeast) here at about 2.0 miles, with pines on both sides but the landscape becoming increasingly marshy to the right (south).

As you progress, a pond and its dammed outflow will come into view straight ahead while to your right is slow-moving water interspersed with marsh grasses. The trail now curves right (east) over the grassy dam. Here you have a good vantage point of the pond, and if you look across to the other shore and up the bank, you'll see the parking lot in the distance.

After crossing the dam and walking through a small grassy area away from the pond shore that's now to your left (north), you'll enter a footpath back under dense, towering pines. Make a short, steep climb and then level off along a ridgeline, with hemlock and pine to your right. You'll see the pond through dense tree cover at 2.5 miles, and from here it's increasingly apparent that you're following the pond shore at a distance, getting more water views through the trees.

Before too long, you'll decrease in elevation rapidly, walking down closer to the pond's edge. This section is much less rutted and doesn't seem to get much foot traffic. Cross a brook at about 2.7 miles into a field, where you want to bear right (northeast) to follow the tree line that bears up to the right. The trail is actually a tractor path through the field that begins a steady shift toward the left (northwest). Bear left (northwest) and continue following the tractor road down through large yet wide-open pine forest before making a steady climb up through a meadow.

When you see the brown wooden signboard up ahead, you'll know that you're returning to the parking lot, completing the loop.

Miles and Directions

0.0 Turn left (southwest) onto Route 94 and walk downhill to the trailhead.

0.2 Turn right (west) onto an unmarked, narrow trail just before utility pole 33½.

0.4 Turn left (south) at a four-way intersection, heading down a rutted hill.

0.5 Turn right (west) at an intersection with a disused wood road.

0.8 Bear left (south) at an intersection in a grassy clearing overlooking the marsh.

1.0 Curve to the left (east) at a Y intersection.

1.2 Turn left (south) to make a steep climb up a hill.

1.3 After reaching the top of a steep ridge and following the trail to the left, turn right (south) at the top of the hill.

1.4 Bear left (southeast) at a Y intersection.

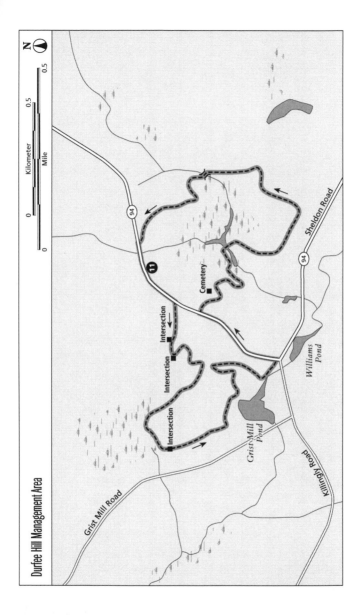

Durfee Hill Management Area

1.5 Turn left (northeast) at a three-way intersection with the brook to your right to walk on Route 94.

1.7 Turn right (east), crossing Route 94 and continuing behind an orange metal gate.

1.8 Cross a sandy clearing, walk up a berm, and then turn left (east) to walk down through a narrow passage to a wood road. Turn left (northeast) toward a large pond.

2.1 Turn right (east) to pass over a dam; then follow the trail up onto a ridge that follows the contour of the pond.

2.7 Cross a brook into a field and follow the tree line bearing up to the right (northeast). Follow the tractor path up toward the parking area.

3.1 Arrive back at your car.

12 Mount Tom Trail

This hike up and over Mount Tom, in the vast Arcadia Management Area, features a wide variety of hiking conditions and scenery. You'll pass under towering red pines, cross swift-moving trout streams, and pause atop rocky cliffs with long panoramic views.

Distance: 5.4-mile loop
Approximate hiking time: 3.5 hours
Difficulty: Moderate
Elevation gain: 333 feet
Trail surface: Gravel and sand access roads, dirt footpaths, rock ledges
Best season: Apr–Oct
Other trail users: Cross-country skiers, snowshoers, mountain bikers, anglers

Canine compatibility: Dogs must be on leash at all times
Permits and fees: None
Schedule: Open year-round from 5:00 a.m. to sunset
Maps: TOPO! New England
Trail contact: State of Rhode Island DEM—Division of Parks & Recreation Headquarters, 1100 Tower Hill Rd., North Kingstown, RI 02852; (401) 667-6200; www .riparks.com

Finding the trailhead: From Route 3 southwest of Providence, take Route 165 (Mount Tom Road) west for 4 miles. Look for a sign marking the ARCADIA CHECK STATION AND CANOE access to your left (south), take the left at that sign. Restrooms at parking area.

The Hike

As soon as you enter the trailhead parking lot, down a short dirt road, you'll see a relatively new picnic pavilion to your left (east) and a toilet facility straight ahead. A white paint square on a pine tree at the back right of the parking area marks the trailhead.

The trail begins on flat, sandy terrain surrounded by towering red pine. This initial stretch, over a grassy area, is well marked with white blazes. The forest is wide open with very little underbrush. Curve left (south) through a forest reminiscent of a pine barren with two layers of coniferous trees at 0.3 mile, following the white markings. Continue on a wide grassy footpath. You'll notice that the grass extends out into the forest floor and underbrush is almost nonexistent.

Turn sharply to the right (west) at 0.5 mile, abruptly transitioning from being exclusively surrounded by red pine to having a mix of cherry, oak, and swamp maple to your left (south) while thick red pine groves continue to your right (north). The trail surface remains a flat and wide access road. Turn left (south), continuing to follow the white blazes, onto a dirt access road. At about the 0.7-mile mark you'll see a wooden bridge crossing Parris Brook straight ahead. Just before the bridge you'll see a small brown sign with white lettering to your right, indicating that this is the Mount Tom Trail. You will bear right back onto the trail just before the bridge. Do not cross it.

Turn right (west) down a narrow footpath through underbrush, paralleling the river to your left (south). Soon the water's edge will be immediately to your left. The trail bed is low lying and may be wet, depending on the weather and season.

Pass a small waterfall at 0.8 mile, which cascades over a several-foot-tall dam. It's apparent that this spot is also prime for fly-fishing due to the well-worn path leading up to it. Continue paralleling the stream, surrounded by underbrush and pine. Turn left (west) at 0.9 mile onto Mount Tom Road, walking a short distance down the road before turning right (northwest) into the woods, following the white blazes through a mix of red pine and small oaks. You'll be climbing up a small incline built up with log steps to prevent erosion.

The trail continues, a wide footpath over mostly sand, and soon levels out with a stone wall off to your left (west). To your right, you'll notice that you're on a ridge rising out of the forest floor, allowing you some wooded views.

Begin walking on a rock ledge high above the forest floor at 1.2 miles. Soon you'll wind away from the edge of this cliff into the interior of the woods, passing through a wet spot before climbing up onto a larger ridge increasing in elevation. Here you'll begin having some great views, and you'll enjoy the first overlook on this route, with views of the horizon. From here, you'll progress on the rock ledge away from the cliff's edge, winding along the ledge. Depart back into the woods off the ledge as you near the 1.3-mile mark, where you'll make a short but steep descent back to a mixed forest of mostly small saplings.

Turn left (north) sharply at about 1.4 miles, continuing to follow the white-blazed trail along another ridge within the woods. Soon you'll be scrambling up rock again, as this ridge rises above the tree line and provides the same type of views you had earlier. The trail surface is a mix of rock and earth surrounded by small oak and pine. Be sure to try out several stone chairs and a table built into the rock ledge at 1.6 miles, a resting place from ridge-walking.

From the rest area, the trail mostly follows the ridgeline to about the 1.9-mile mark where it begins a steep descent down to Route 165, which is now audible below. As soon as you reach the roadside, look across the pavement to the left (northwest), and you'll see a stone with a white marking indicating where the trail continues after crossing.

As soon as you cross, you'll see the MOUNT TOM trail sign marking the spot where you'll climb up a rutted-out rock scramble into the forest, through small- to medium-size oak. Continue to wind through low-lying blueberry bushes for as far as the eye can see.

Continue following the White Trail to your left (northwest); at 2.2 miles, you'll come to a three-way intersection where you'll bear right (east) then left (northeast) to cut across an old logging road then along a long straightaway through recently logged forest. The trail surface continues to be completely flat and is now a sandy footpath headed through seemingly endless blueberry groves. Soon you'll see a garage through the trees to your left (west), and here the trail is notably straight, narrow, and sandy into the distance. Denser underbrush including laurel begins surrounding the trail at 2.4 miles, and soon the laurel figures prominently on either side of the route, some towering over the trail.

Continue straight (northwest) on the White Trail through another four-way intersection at 2.8 miles, and soon you'll see a stone wall off to your left (west) in the woods paralleling the trail. Behind this wall, the trees have recently been logged, which over time will likely give way to wildflowers, blueberries, and then a renewal of forest growth, principally a mix of pine and oak.

Head down a slight grade before reaching an intersection with a dirt road at 3.1 miles. You'll see that the White Trail continues across the dirt road in front of you. Turn right (east) here, onto the sandy dirt road (the Barber Trail), departing from the White Trail. There will be blueberry bushes mostly to your right (south), and the road begins its gradual but long descent. As you walk, you'll see rolling hills in the distance and a meadow that pitches downward in the foreground.

Before too long, cross a stream running through a culvert underneath the road. You'll also see that the field continues to be visible through the woods to your left (north). As soon as the field ends, denser pine surrounds the road as you continue walking down a steady decline. Upon passing straight through a brown metal gate at 4.5 miles, you'll see a small parking area to your right (south). You'll now be on a completely level grade surrounded by a mixed forest with no views.

After about another 100 yards, reach another intersection with a brown metal gate to your right (south). Cross over a wooden bridge crossing Flat River (you are now on a blue-blazed trail) and turn right (south), continuing on the dirt road. Cross another wooden bridge at 4.7 miles, over the same river but farther downstream. This bridge spans a deep pool that appears to be a great fishing spot.

Pass straight through another intersection at 4.8 miles, and soon you'll pass a stately red pine grove high up on a hillside to your right. At 5.0 miles pass another intersection, where you'll see a large parking lot through the trees straight ahead. Turn right (southwest) here, passing around a metal gate. Car traffic on Route 165, down in the distance, will now be audible. Pass through dense pine saplings on a wood road covered with mostly grass back to the roadside. Turn right (west) and walk along Route 165, crossing the bridge that you previously drove across, and turn left (south) into the parking lot entrance, returning to your car.

Miles and Directions

0.0 The trail begins on a flat, sandy trail bed marked with a white paint square on a pine tree.

0.3 Bear left (south), entering a pine barren–like forest with two layers of conifers.

0.5 Turn right (west) sharply.

0.7 Turn left (south) onto a dirt access road; then bear right back onto the trail just before a wooden bridge crossing Parris Brook (do not cross the bridge).

0.8 Pass a small waterfall.

0.9 Turn left (west) at the intersection with Mount Tom Road; then turn right (northwest) into the woods on the White Trail.

1.2 Walk on a rock ledge above the forest floor; then pass the first overlook. Head down off the ledge back into the woods briefly before climbing back up.

1.6 Pass several stone chairs and a table built into the rock ledge. Continue mostly along the ridgeline.

1.9 Make a steep descent; then cross Route 165.

2.2 Continue following the White Trail at a three-way intersection by bearing right then left to cut across an old logging road.

2.4 Head into denser underbrush, including laurel that towers over the trail.

2.8 Continue straight on the White Trail through another four-way intersection.

3.1 Head down a slight grade to an intersection with a dirt road and turn right (east) on the dirt road. This is the Barber Trail.

4.5 Pass through a brown metal gate; there will be a parking area to the right. About 100 yards later, cross a wooden bridge spanning the Flat River; then turn right (south) onto a dirt road following blue blazes.

4.7 Cross a wooden bridge spanning a deep pool.

4.8 Pass straight through an intersection.

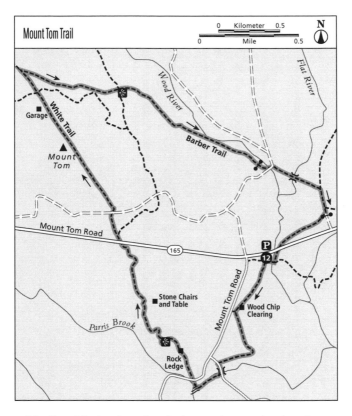

5.0 Turn right (southwest) at the intersection, passing through a metal gate.

5.4 Return back to your car.

13 Breakheart Trail

Another route within the vast Arcadia Management Area, the Breakheart Trail passes through extensive forest, wide-open fields, and marsh. You'll also skirt around the remnants of an abandoned youth camp now reduced to mostly stone foundations. Toward the end of the route, you'll pass under the Breakheart Pond spillway, a popular fishing access point.

Distance: 5.9-mile loop

Approximate hiking time: 3 hours

Difficulty: Moderate

Elevation gain: 310 feet

Trail surface: Wood roads, footpaths

Best season: Apr–Oct

Other trail users: Cross-country skiers, snowshoers, ATVs, anglers

Canine compatibility: Dogs must be on leash at all times

Permits and fees: None

Schedule: Open year-round from 5:00 a.m. to sunset

Maps: TOPO! New England

Trail contact: State of Rhode Island DEM–Division of Parks & Recreation Headquarters, 1100 Tower Hill Rd., North Kingstown, RI 02852; (401) 667-6200; www .riparks.com

Finding the trailhead: From Route 3 southwest of Providence, follow Route 165 west for 3.4 miles, turning right (north) at the West Exeter Baptist Church onto Frosty Hollow Road. Follow this gravel road until it ends at a T intersection, with a nonvehicular wood road heading up into the woods straight ahead. Turn left (west), continuing on a dirt road; although it's unmarked, you are now on Plain Road. Continue past a sign marking the entrance to FISH AND WILDLIFE EDUCATION OFFICES to your right (north), and immediately after crossing a small wooden bridge over a brook, pull over to the side of the road into a sandy turnout large enough for approximately two cars. The trail begins here, paralleling the stream you just crossed.

The Hike

Begin on the white-blazed Shelter Trail, walking through a mix of dense medium-size white and red pine and paralleling a stream seen at a distance through the trees. A nice and easy amble on a wide footpath carpeted with pine needles. From here, the trail gradually declines into deeper forest. Turn left (west) at a T intersection not far from the clearing, continuing to follow the white-blazed trail.

You'll be traveling through mostly pine and quickly reach a steep hill with log steps built into the slope to control erosion. Upon reaching the top of this hill at about 0.4 mile, you'll pass an abandoned red building immediately to your left (south). Most of the other structures of what was once a youth camp have been reduced to foundations on either side of the trail, interspersed with thick groves of small red pine. Soon you will reach a clearing with a stone chimney and foundation to your left, which appears to be all that remains of a lodge. Continue on this flat-graded segment of the Shelter Trail, passing through a clearing on its right edge and back into mostly pine.

At about 0.6 mile turn right (northeast) at a four-way intersection—what appears to be the camp's center—continuing to follow the White Trail. You are now on a narrow footpath passing through a mix of scrub, red, and white pine on a relatively straight and flat grade. Different-sized oaks soon figure prominently into the mix.

At 0.8 mile, you will come to a trail that cuts off to the left; continue straight.

The trail straddles an overgrown wooded marsh to your right (east) and a steep incline of dense, mostly oak forest to your left (west). Turn right (east) at a T intersection onto the Yellow Trail (a.k.a. Breakheart Trail) as you near the 1.4-mile mark, winding alongside a steep incline of dense pine to your immediate left and wooded marsh down a small embankment to your right.

Continue through small pine groves along the low-lying forest floor, level with the wooded swamp, until crossing a brook over a long footbridge at 1.6 miles. Shortly after the crossing you'll transition to drier ground, passing through a stately mix of white and red pine on a wide-open needle-blanketed forest floor. Cross Phillips Brook, a swift-flowing medium-size river, at 1.8 miles, using a second wooden footbridge. After crossing, climb up a slight but steady incline to higher ground, away from the presence of wooded swamp.

Towering pines stretching up to the sky let the sunlight in and allow for a wide-open forest floor that is grassy in patches. You'll follow a grassy trail bed along a ridge at a slight decline. The trail bed carves into this grassy ridge as you continue downward. As soon as the trail levels off, you'll begin making a steep climb up an embankment, away from a low-lying wooded area that is down in a small valley.

The trail follows along the Acid Factory Brook for a bit and then crosses it on a wooden footbridge at 2.4 miles. The trail carves into a steep bank with water views directly below to your right. The trail is now an old logging or access road instead of a footpath. At about the 2.5-mile mark, bear left (north) to follow the yellow blazes; even though it's tempting to continue straight on the established wood road, make this turn onto a rougher footpath.

Making a steady climb through small pine, oak, and beech, you'll be moving farther from the riverbed and passing over a mix of rugged terrain on flat stretches punctuated with several short, steep hills. At 2.7 miles you will reach another intersection. Continue straight to follow the yellow blazes. Turn left at a T intersection at about 3.1 miles and then make a quick right, continuing on the Yellow Trail.

Soon you'll see Breakheart Brook paralleling the trail to your left (east), with a stone wall separating you from the water. At 4.0 miles turn left (east) at a T intersection then over a wooden footbridge to continue on the yellow-blazed trail. The bridge itself offers a good vantage point of the brook coursing through a marsh and emptying into the pond below.

At 4.1 miles, bear right (west) at the top of a small rise. The pond shore will be barely visible at times through the trees to your right. You'll soon notice you're getting closer to the water's edge because less underbrush and larger pines separating you from the water are enabling these views.

Cross a brook over a wooden bridge at about 4.6 miles; then turn right (west) about 100 feet later onto an old dirt road, and soon you'll see a stone foundation overlooking the pond to your right. Remember to keep paralleling and progressing ever closer to the pond shore, staying on the established wood road. Soon you'll see a red metal gate in the distance. After passing around this gate, cross a bridge at the base of a concrete spillway outfitted with a now decrepit fish ladder at 4.8 miles. After crossing, turn left (west), down a dirt road and away from the spillway, following the road to a four-way intersection at Plain Road at the 5.3-mile mark. Continue straight (west) down Plain Road, the dirt road you initially drove in on, following it back to where you parked your car.

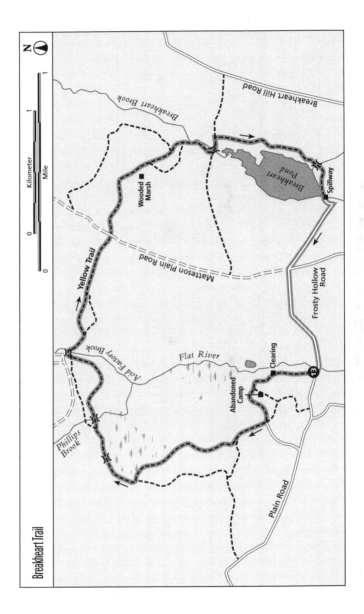

Breakheart Trail

Miles and Directions

0.0 Begin on the white-blazed Shelter Trail, to your right (north) at the edge of the sandy parking turnout.

0.2 Descend into deeper forest; then turn left (west) at T intersection, continuing on the white-blazed trail.

0.4 Pass by a red former youth camp building.

0.6 Turn right (northeast) at four-way intersection and continue following the White Trail.

1.4 Turn right (east) at T intersection onto the Yellow Trail (a.k.a. Breakheart Trail).

1.6 Cross a brook on a long footbridge.

1.8 Cross a second wooden footbridge over Phillips Brook.

2.4 Cross a wooden footbridge over Acid Factory Brook; then continue on the Yellow Trail.

2.5 Bear left at a Y intersection to remain on the yellow-blazed trail.

2.7 At a four-way intersection, keep straight to remain on yellow-blazed trail.

3.1 Turn left (north) at a T intersection with Matteson Plain Road and then make a quick right (east), continuing on the Yellow Trail.

4.0 Turn left (east) at a T intersection (still yellow blazed) over a wooden footbridge.

4.1 Bear right (west) at top of a small rise.

4.6 Cross a brook over a wooden bridge; then about 100 feet later, turn right onto dirt road.

4.8 Cross a bridge at the base of the concrete spillway; then turn left (west) down a dirt road away from the spillway.

5.3 Continue straight at four-way intersection to follow Plain Road.

5.9 Return to your car.

14 Ben Utter Trail

Another route within Rhode Island's 14,000-acre Arcadia Management Area, the Ben Utter Trail passes close by Wood River up to Stepstone Falls, passing mill ruins and massive quarried stones. The return leg passes high above the river through mixed forest.

Distance: 2.8-mile lollipop

Approximate hiking time: 2.5 hours

Difficulty: Moderate

Elevation gain: 190 feet

Trail surface: Wood roads and footpaths

Best season: Apr–Oct

Other trail users: Cross-country skiers, snowshoers

Canine compatibility: Dogs must be on leash at all times

Permits and fees: None

Schedule: Open year-round from 5:00 a.m. to sunset

Maps: TOPO! New England

Trail contact: State of Rhode Island DEM–Division of Parks & Recreation Headquarters, 1100 Tower Hill Rd., North Kingstown, RI 02852; (401) 667-6200; www .riparks.com

Finding the trailhead: From Route 3 southwest of Providence, follow Route 165 west for 3.4 miles, turning right (north) at the West Exeter Baptist Church onto Frosty Hollow Road. Follow this gravel road until it ends at a T intersection, with a nonvehicular wood road heading up into the woods straight ahead. Turn left (west) on a dirt road; although it's unmarked, you are now on Plain Road. Continue past a sign marking the FISH AND WILDLIFE EDUCATION OFFICES entrance to your right (north) and cross a small wooden bridge over a brook (the parking area for Breakheart Pond is just beyond). Continue following Plain Road until you cross a second wooden bridge. Parking for the trailhead is immediately to your right (north) after the crossing, in a sand and gravel turnout. There's space for about five cars.

The Hike

The yellow-blazed trail begins at the parking turnout, paralleling the Wood River close to your right (east) on the northwest side of a wooden bridge. Pine trees tower over the trail, mostly to your right and on the river's opposite shore, while deciduous trees populate the woods to your left.

Continue on a flat grade. Even though the trail is well marked, it can be confusing since you'll see both blue and yellow blazes next to each other and, at points, numerous herd paths. Cross a wooden footbridge over a small, wooded swamp close to the river's edge at 0.1 mile. Soon you'll notice the beginning of a fork in the river, with a narrow, wooded island in the center, thought to have once been a millrace, at 0.2 mile. A smaller stream is closest to the trail, while the main river swiftly flows on the other side of this island.

Shortly, you'll reach an intersection where you turn left (northwest), heading up a steep but short hill over rocks on log steps built into the hillside, moving away from the river's edge on the Yellow/Blue Trail. Almost as soon as you climb up, you'll head down the hill to once more parallel the river's edge. At 0.3 mile the trail comes to a road with a wooden fence section where you'll follow the Yellow/Blue Trail to the right (northeast). Follow this trail through laurel groves.

After crossing a wooden footbridge, the laurel surrounding the trail gets denser and taller. You can still hear the river through the trees to your right and catch glimpses of water every so often, but you now aren't nearly as close to it as during the first segment of this route. Cross a footbridge over a stream at 0.5 mile, continuing over a stony trail bed through mostly oak, birch, and maple. Soon you'll see mill ruin sites to your left (west) marked with large stone blocks that were at one point a sawmill.

Cross another footbridge over a small stream that empties into the river close by to your right at 0.6 mile. A little farther, you'll see another vestige of a mill, a stone dam in the river creating a large pool behind it. After passing these ruins you'll be walking on a stony trail bed away from the river, through beech ranging from midgrowth to sapling along with massive oaks. Depending on the season and amount of precipitation, you'll cross wet muddy spots, but you'll have plenty of stones to step over these areas to keep your feet dry.

At 1.0 mile reach an intersection where you turn right (northeast) onto the Blue Trail (the Ben Utter Trail goes off to the left), which is a narrow footpath passing through light-growth deciduous trees. As you progress, the stones littering the trail bed become boulders, matching the riverbed that's becoming ever more visible to your right (east) once more.

You'll cross over large blocks of stone that appear as if they have been pieced together like a gigantic patio and soon see a wooden footbridge to the right (east) at 1.2 miles. By this point, there are multiple herd paths from visitors wandering along the water's edge. Follow the trail to the bridge; then cross to the other shore and turn left (north) heading toward Falls River Road. The bridge is a perfect scenic viewing spot because you'll see the Stepstone Falls in the distance, up to your left (north). As you walk north, the river is now to your left (west).

Shortly, you'll have some more river-viewing opportunities amid piles of large stone blocks that were quarried and left behind. The telltale signs of this activity are mechanized hatch marks chipped into the rock. The trail surface continues to be large flat slabs of rock interspersed with remarkably straight line or gradually curving cracks at different intervals.

Soon, you'll be standing directly above the falls with a pile of large stone blocks that look like they were carved out as foundation stone immediately to your left. Several steps beyond, at about 1.4 miles, the trail intersects Falls River Road. Turn left (west) onto this road and cross the river on a concrete bridge. Quickly take another left (south) turn, down through a sand and gravel parking area onto the Yellow Trail. Now you will be paralleling the river (to your left/east) at a higher elevation on a wood road. The river is visible through the trees but farther away than before.

The trail, which seems to have once been a wagon road, continues climbing up and away from the river at a slight grade. The woods are mostly deciduous, punctuated with large oak.

Continue straight on the yellow portion of the Ben Utter Trail, passing a red pavilion to your left on a level plateau within the woods at 1.7 miles. Soon after, at 1.8 miles, bear left (southeast) just before a road to follow the trail as it parallels the road on your right and the stream below to your left.

At about 2.5 miles you'll come to the intersection marked by the wooden fence section you came to previously, thereby closing the loop. Bear right (southeast) to follow the trail back to the parking area.

Miles and Directions

0.0 Begin on yellow-blazed section of the Ben Utter Trail.

0.1 Cross a wooden footbridge over wooded swamp close to the river's edge.

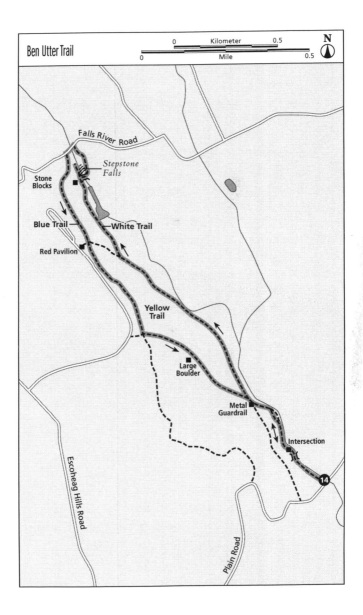

Ben Utter Trail

Stepstone Falls

Stone Blocks

Blue Trail

White Trail

Red Pavilion

Yellow Trail

Large Boulder

Metal Guardrail

Intersection

Falls River Road

Escoheag Hills Road

Plain Road

14

N

Kilometer
0   0.5
Mile
0   0.5

0.3 Trail reaches a road and wooden fence section; bear right (northeast) to follow the Yellow/Blue Trail.

0.5 Cross a footbridge over a stream.

0.6 Cross another footbridge.

1.0 Turn right (northeast) onto the Blue Trail (the Ben Utter Trail goes to the left).

1.2 Follow the trail right (east) to a wooden bridge that crosses the stream. After crossing, turn left (north) to walk toward Falls River Road.

1.4 Turn left onto Falls River Road, cross the bridge, and then turn left again through a sand and gravel parking area and follow the Yellow Trail that becomes a wood road.

1.7 Pass a red pavilion and continue on the Ben Utter Trail (Yellow Trail).

1.8 Bear left (southeast) just before a road to follow the trail paralleling the road.

2.5 Return to intersection marked by a section of wooden fence to close the loop. Follow the trail (southeast) toward the parking area.

2.8 Return back to your car.

15 Carolina South Loop

This route passes through open meadows, dense pine forest, and past two historical cemeteries. The majority of the first half of this route is immersed in a wide-open overgrown meadow where, in some spots, rye and other grasses are planted to attract wildlife.

Distance: 3.1-mile loop
Approximate hiking time: 2 hours
Difficulty: Easy
Elevation gain: 64 feet
Trail surface: Wood roads and footpaths
Best season: Apr–Oct
Other trail users: Cross-country skiers, snowshoers
Canine compatibility: Dogs must be on leash at all times

Permits and fees: None
Schedule: Open year-round from sunrise to sunset
Maps: TOPO! New England; map board near trailhead
Trail contact: State of Rhode Island DEM–Division of Parks & Recreation Headquarters, 1100 Tower Hill Rd., North Kingstown, RI 02852; (401) 667-6200; www .riparks.com

Finding the trailhead: From I-95 south of Providence, take exit 3A northbound or 3B southbound onto Route 138 east. After several miles, turn right (south) on Route 112 and travel 2.5 miles to Pine Hill Road. Turn right (west) on Pine Hill Road and proceed 1.5 miles to the parking area on your left (south). The lot is surrounded by meadows, and a red hunter check-in station that is no longer used is on the left.

The Hike

From the small sand and gravel parking area, you will see a modest historical cemetery in a field to your right (west) as you're facing away from the road. Pass around a red metal gate, walking a short distance on a dirt road into a field, where you'll see the hunter check-in station, a concrete-block building painted red, and a brown signboard with a small trail map.

Turn left (east) onto a gravel access road that begins in a meadow and continues into the woods where the trail begins a long, straight, southward stretch. Depending on the season, you'll be able to look to your right (west) on this portion and see a wide variety of wildflowers. The woods that soon rise up on either side are populated with two extremes, either tiny or towering red pine. Though, you will notice recent logging activity in the woods to the left (east), which creates more wildflower habitat as the open areas grow over. A narrow strip of forest to your right (west) separates you from the field that you parallel, and the trail lies on a flat grade blanketed in pine needles.

You'll make the transition to mostly deciduous midgrowth maple at 0.4 mile, beginning a slight decline. Shortly after, you'll enter a field, one of many in a series to come, containing seasonal wildflowers with a few oaks to your right. The access road continues flat, passing through intervals of forest and field in rapid succession. The longest stretch of field, at 0.8 mile, contains patches planted with rye and other grasses to attract wildlife.

Depart from this series of fields at 1.1 miles, passing into forest composed of a mix of large red pine and deciduous trees, mostly medium-size swamp maple and small oak.

Turn left (northeast) at a T intersection at 1.2 miles onto a wide trail, where a band of large red pine separates you from a field behind them in the distance. As you walk, these trees will be immediately to your right (south). Follow this trail for about a tenth of a mile until you see a small footpath breaking off to the left (east) just as the main trail bends right (south). This small path is short, and beyond it you can see a massive field through the trees. Take this path.

Once in the field, follow alongside the brushy woods line to your left (northwest). You'll see that this area is part of a working sod farm and is actively tilled.

Follow the woods line until you reach a small, grassy footpath that bears off to the left (northeast) at about 1.5 miles. Off to the right you'll see a pile of aged lumber and rubble that was once a barn. Bear left (east) onto the grassy footpath where you will also see a series of wood posts marked with blue blazes to the right and woods to the left, the contour of which the grassy path follows. You will soon see two more posts with blue blazes to your left.

Enter the woods onto the Blue Trail (a.k.a. the National Scenic Trail [NST]) at 1.6 miles, and soon you'll enter an extensive pine forest with needles carpeting a trail that is larger than a footpath but not quite a wood road. Depart this grand pine forest at 1.8 miles, passing into a woodland of pine and oak.

At 2.1 miles you'll notice that a newer section of trail parallels what appears to be the original trail bed but is now an eroded drainage ditch. Shortly after this spot, the Blue Trail curves sharply into the pine forest, up a steady but gradual incline where you'll reach an old cemetery surrounded by a white picket fence at about 2.2 miles.

After checking out the headstones, break out into a clearing, and the forest transitions into mixed deciduous trees and pine. Continue following the blue blazes to where the trail splits at 2.4 miles. Here, the forest has noticeably opened up, both in the canopy and on the floor with grassy patches

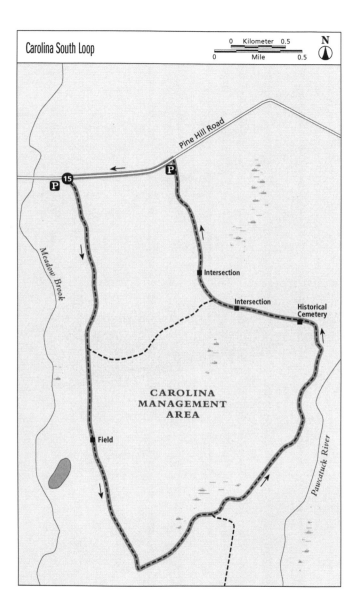

Carolina South Loop

0 Kilometer 0.5

0 Mile 0.5

N

Pine Hill Road

P 15

P

Meadow Brook

Intersection

Intersection

Historical Cemetery

Pawcatuck River

CAROLINA MANAGEMENT AREA

Field

between trees that are spaced farther apart. Follow the blue-blazed trail to the right (northeast). After this intersection the trail will remain flat and once again head back into a thick pine forest containing some massive trees.

You'll reach a small dirt parking lot right off Pine Hill Road at 2.9 miles. Pass through this parking area, heading to Pine Hill Road. Turn left (west) onto this road and walk back to the parking lot.

Miles and Directions

0.0 Begin behind a red metal gate; then quickly turn left to follow the trail into the woods where it flows steadily south.

0.8 Pass through long stretch of field.

1.1 Depart from fields into forest.

1.2 Turn left (northeast) at a T intersection; then turn left onto a small footpath leading to a massive field.

1.6 Enter the woods on the Blue Trail.

1.8 Depart from a grand pine forest.

2.1 Pass along a newer section of trail; then pass an old cemetery surrounded by a white picket fence.

2.4 Bear right (northeast) on the Blue Trail at a fork.

2.9 Reach a small dirt parking lot off Pine Hill Road; then follow the road to the left (west).

3.1 Return to your car.

16 Great Swamp Management Area

One of the largest preserved marshlands in Rhode Island, this hike takes you into the heart of all the bird-watching action. From ospreys to warblers, numerous waterfowl, and beaver are just some of the species that call these lands home.

Distance: 4.5-mile lollipop
Approximate hiking time: 1.5 hours
Difficulty: Easy
Elevation gain: 105 feet
Trail surface: Gravel and grass access roads
Best season: Apr–Oct
Other trail users: Cross-country skiers, snowshoers, mountain bikers
Canine compatibility: Dogs must be on leash at all times

Permits and fees: None
Schedule: Open year-round sunrise to sunset
Maps: TOPO! New England; map on signboard near trailhead
Trail contact: State of Rhode Island DEM—Division of Parks & Recreation Headquarters, 1100 Tower Hill Rd., North Kingstown, RI 02852; (401) 667-6200; www.riparks.com

Finding the trailhead: From the Providence area, take I-95 south to Route 138 east. Follow Route 138 to West Kingston. The great swamp management area sign will be to your right (south) just before crossing a bridge and reaching the intersection of Route 110. (If approaching from the east on Route 138, the great swamp management sign will be just beyond the intersection with Route 110, over the bridge.) Turn south onto Liberty Lane; follow this road until it ends at a railroad track. Turn sharply to the left (southwest) onto a dirt road, Great Neck Road, and follow until it dead-ends in a large dirt parking lot. You will pass a maintenance facility and rifle range en route.

The Hike

The trail begins behind a brown metal gate, heading down a flat and sandy access road. Pass a signboard with map; then walk through a mixed deciduous woodland of mostly swamp maple. The roadbed is the only elevation separating you from wooded swamp on either side, with a trail surface of pressed stone dust and gravel giving it the texture of asphalt.

Soon you'll have views alternating between wide-open marsh and low-lying brush. A drainage pipe runs underneath the roadbed at about 0.3 mile, connecting the open marsh that you'll now see on both sides of the trail. This is a great scenic viewpoint, particularly for the sheer diversity of marsh grasses and birdlife if you linger long enough and bring binoculars. To your left, you'll have marginally obstructed views of marsh far into the distance. Pass over a patch of loose gravel in this spot before returning to a hard-packed trail surface.

Shortly after this gravel patch, bear right (southwest) at a fork in the access road marked with a monument stone dedicated to Dr. John Mulleady. Now you'll be heading away from marsh surroundings into low-lying forest of mostly swamp maple and underbrush scattered with some large pines. Soon you'll be climbing up a slight grade into drier woods that will have you forgetting you are indeed in the middle of the Great Swamp preserve. Pass a stand of large red pines to your right (west), and soon a meadow will open up next to the trail on your right (west). As you progress, you'll be headed toward a much larger, wide-open field to your right. Upon reaching this meadow, you'll recognize its magnitude as it extends away from the trail's edge to your right for a stretch. To your left, large oaks populate the forest.

After passing this long field, walk directly under power lines until you reach a Y intersection at 0.8 mile. Turn right (northwest) onto a grassy wood road, walking away from the power lines and traveling through mostly oak mixed with small maple and holly bushes. At 1.0 mile this access road passes up onto a grassy dike containing the Great Swamp to your left (south).

From here to the 2.5-mile mark you'll be walking along a flat, grassy road on top of the dike, with continual wide-open marsh views providing you with plenty of bird- and wildlife-viewing opportunities. Several osprey nesting platforms are visible in the distance within the swamp. Down below to your right, dense underbrush and swamp maple fringe the mown-grass edge.

Soon you'll parallel the power line that you passed under previously; only now it's to your left (south), spanning the marsh. The dike curves up to the left (south) at 1.9 miles, spanning the swamp's eastern shore up toward where the power lines cross the roadbed at 2.1 miles. Standing here, looking out into the marsh, you'll see an old wooden platform/walkway, possibly built for utility maintenance, that at one time connected the shore with the first set of telephone poles out in the water. Now they are tumbled down and impassable.

From here, the marsh will continue close by to your left (east), until, at 2.5 miles, you'll leave the dike and swamp to climb into the forest. You'll also have a chance to rest on a stone seat overlooking the marsh next to a telephone pole that may have been an osprey platform at one time. The access road makes a steady climb but at a slight grade, through mixed deciduous forest of mostly holly, oak, and hickory.

At 2.7 miles, you'll pass fields both to your left and right. The field to your right (east) appears to be cultivated, while to your left, it's mostly meadow grass and underbrush. Here, the trail levels off and straightens out, passing through many different-size swamp maples. Off in the distance, down through the field to your left, you'll get some glimpses of the Great Swamp.

Turn left (northwest) at a three-way intersection at 2.9 miles, where the trail widens and meadow continues in spots to your left. To your right, quite a few holly bushes will be interspersed with the swamp maples. This landscape will transition to field. At about 3.3 miles you'll cross underneath the power lines, paralleling them to your right (southeast), until you reach the intersection where you previously headed down to the Great Swamp, completing the loop. Continue straight (northeast) through this intersection and retrace your steps back to your car.

Miles and Directions

0.0 Begin behind a brown metal gate, heading down a flat and sandy access road.

0.3 Cross a drainage pipe.

0.8 Turn right (northwest) at a Y intersection onto a grassy wood road.

1.0. The access road passes up onto a grassy dike containing the Great Swamp.

1.9 Curve left on the dike, following the swamp's eastern shore.

2.1 Cross under power lines.

2.5 Leave the dike and swamp as you climb into the forest. Pass a stone seat overlooking the marsh.

2.7 Pass through fields.

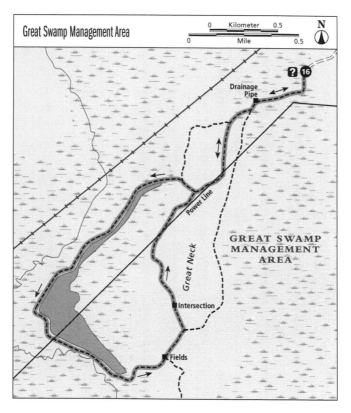

2.9 Turn left (northwest) at a three-way intersection.

3.3 Cross underneath the power lines again.

4.5 Return to your car.

17 Napatree Point Conservation Area

One of the largest coastal access points in Rhode Island, the beachfront on the outgoing segment of this loop is wide open and well preserved, with miles of dunes backing soft sand and wide-open ocean. If you come during summer, be sure to bring your bathing suit so you can cool off and relax awhile. This area is also popular with birding enthusiasts since it's within a major migratory path.

Distance: 3.5-mile loop
Approximate hiking time: 2 hours
Difficulty: Easy
Elevation gain: 18 feet
Trail surface: Beach and boulders
Best season: Apr–Oct
Other trail users: Beachcombers, anglers, boaters

Canine compatibility: Dogs must be on leash at all times
Permits and fees: None
Schedule: Coastline open year-round sunrise to sunset
Maps: TOPO! New England
Trail contact: Watch Hill Fire District, 222 Watch Hill Rd., Westerly, RI 02891; (401) 348-6540

Finding the trailhead: From Route 1 in Westerly in the southwestern portion of the state, follow Route 1A south until you reach Watch Hill Road, which forks off to the right (southwest). Follow Watch Hill Road until it runs into Bay Street, which fronts Watch Hill Cove. During the summer, if you're lucky enough to find street parking in Watch Hill, you'll be limited to two hours of free parking. Otherwise, you must pay a fee to park in a lot. Off-season, parking shouldn't be an issue.

The Hike

Begin by walking from your car down Bay Street in Watch Hill, overlooking the harbor directly to your right (north) in the cove. As you're looking out into the little harbor, off to the left (west), across the water in the distance, you'll see a spit of sand and dune grass. This is Napatree Point, and the most straightforward approach to the preserve's entrance is to follow the concrete sidewalk paralleling the water out toward the point. Pass through a parking lot with a low concrete seawall separating you from the water and the boats at their moorings, and continue until you reach sand, passing a chain-link fence to your left (south).

Now you are walking on the beach, with waves lapping several feet away. Turn left (southwest) at a fork in the trail at about 0.3 mile, cutting up through dune grass away from the protected harbor side of the peninsula over to the open ocean. You'll finally see a signboard indicating that this is the Napatree Point Conservation Area.

Wind through dune grass and beach plums up onto a bluff, where you'll get good views of the sandy beach curving up to Napatree Point far in the distance; then head down to the ocean front. From here out to the point you'll be beach walking, with dunes up to your right (north) and ocean to your left (south). Depending on the weather, you'll get some long-distance ocean views.

Most of the dunes and the upper portion of beach to your right is a protected piping plover nesting area, beginning at about 0.7 mile. You'll notice a roped-off area, and during nesting season (spring through midsummer), it's advisable to keep close to the water's edge, away from the ever-watchful plover. Known to be very protective, they will warn you with their shrill call and dive toward your head if they think you're a threat.

As you're walking, particularly next to the surf, you'll notice that the sand is extremely fine grained, with very few stones or pebbles, resulting in a firmly packed surface. It's almost like walking on a soft sidewalk but comfy enough for bare feet.

As you draw closer to the point, you'll see an osprey nesting platform off to your right. Depending on the season, you may see an osprey perched on top. You'll make a sudden and definitive transition to rock and gravel underfoot at 1.5 miles. Large boulders flank the coastline to your left, and to your right, dune grass gives way to beach plum and brushier marsh vegetation. Spectacular and more rugged ocean views abound straight ahead, off the point and to your left. Many people fish on the point, and you'll be doing stone-stepping over rocks surrounded by seaweed and other ocean debris.

Follow the trail right (northeast) up a brief draw to your right at 1.7 miles onto a bluff with thick underbrush. You are now rounding the point where you will see the remnants of Fort Mansfield; then off to the left (northwest) you'll see a breakwater just above the waves and some piers poking through the surface. These are remnants of what once was a summer community before the hurricane of 1938 swept it away.

After rounding the point you'll be headed back toward Watch Hill and will begin to see houses and a water tank on the opposite shore. The terrain remains littered with rocks that extend out into the ocean, making it prime habitat for waterfowl. Most of the larger rocks begin to dissipate into smaller stones, and the shoreline on this side of the peninsula is much weedier and the water more brackish. You'll now have a solid band of marsh grass to your right. If you're walking through here at low tide, you'll notice that the water's edge is cobbled with small stones anchored with grasses growing up between them.

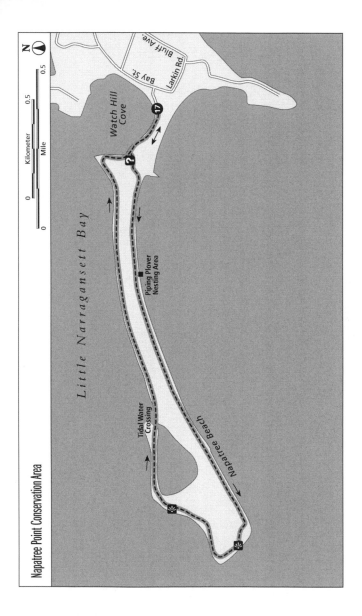

Napatree Point Conservation Area

You will have a full view of Watch Hill Cove (straight ahead/to the east) at 2.1 miles. A marsh pond will be to your right (south) behind the beach head, and dune grasses become the prominent vegetation once again. From here the beach widens, with some more sand, but it still remains unsuitable to swimming due to the small rocks that continue to fringe the shoreline. You'll have clearer views of the harbor at about 2.5 miles and a wider beach with more sand, even though it remains brackish and unfit for swimming. Here you'll also have to cross a shallow tidal stream, by either taking your shoes off during warmer weather or making sure you have tall waterproof boots during colder months.

Upon crossing, the beach improves slightly in quality but remains pebbly and soft, slowing down your pace. You'll still have seaweed-encrusted rocks separating you from the water. As you progress, you'll round corners, putting Watch Hill into ever-closer view, until you complete the loop and retrace your steps back to the car.

Miles and Directions

0.0 Begin by following the concrete sidewalk paralleling the harbor to your right (north).

0.3 Turn left (southwest) at the fork in the trail, heading down the ocean side of the peninsula.

0.7 Pass the beginning of the roped-off piping plover nesting area.

1.5 The trail surface transitions to rock and gravel.

1.7 Round the point, climbing along boulders on a bluff.

2.1 Enjoy a full view of Watch Hill Cove.

2.5 Cross the tidal stream.

3.5 Return to your car.

18 Burlingame North Management Area

This route passes through thick pine groves both at the beginning and middle of the hike, while much of the remainder passes through low-lying wooded swamp and around vernal pools surrounded by beech and swamp maple. Halfway in you'll pass through a canoe campsite, where you can take a side trail to explore the Pawcatuck River before cutting back into the woods.

Distance: 4.2-mile loop
Approximate hiking time: 2.5 hours
Difficulty: Moderate
Elevation gain: 158 feet
Trail surface: Wood roads and forest footpaths
Best season: Apr–Oct
Other trail users: Beachcombers, anglers, boaters
Canine compatibility: Dogs must be on leash at all times

Permits and fees: None
Schedule: Open year-round sunrise to sunset
Maps: TOPO! New England
Trail contact: State of Rhode Island DEM—Division of Parks & Recreation Headquarters, 1100 Tower Hill Rd., North Kingstown, RI 02852; (401) 667-6200; www .riparks.com

Finding the trailhead: From I-95 take exit 93, the last one in Connecticut. Drive south on RI 216 for about 4 miles to Buckeye Brook Road. Turn left (east) and follow Buckeye Brook Road for approximately 1.5 miles; turn left into a small sandy parking area under the cover of pines (enough for three cars).

The Hike

Begin from the small sandy turnoff behind a brown metal gate, under the cover of large pines on a level wood road—the blue-blazed National Scenic Trail (NST). You'll soon transition into mostly deciduous forest as the roadbed passes through some lower-lying wet spots, depending on the season. After crossing a brook, climb a small hill curving up to your left (west) on a rutted stony road.

Continue to the right (north) on the Blue Trail at a Y intersection at about 0.3 mile. The trail bed is visibly more established and worn, traversing through an even mix of small and large oak, swamp maple, and pine.

Continue straight (north) on the Blue Trail through another intersection at 0.6 mile. Soon after crossing a brook that runs under the road, you'll notice that there are more beech in the mix of trees surrounding the trail, and that a rock ridge extends to your right (east) in the woods, roughly paralleling the trail at a distance. This is the first of many rock outcroppings you'll see poking out of the forest floor in various places along this route.

Continue on flat terrain, and soon a brook (to your right/east through the trees) will parallel the trail. You'll pass a trail spur to your right (east) at 0.8 mile, continuing straight (north) on the Blue Trail before curving slightly to the left (northwest) and then snaking around some large rock outcroppings while making a steady but gradual climb.

At 1.4 miles a wood road juts off to your left (north), but continue straight on the Blue Trail. A little later you'll begin a winding climb through the forest to the 1.6-mile mark where a crucial intersection is noted by a sign that says NORTH SOUTH TRAIL with an arrow pointing to your right.

The blue-blazed access road continues off to your right (north), but you'll want to break away from the blue, making a left (southwest) turn onto the White Trail (no blazes), which is also a wood road.

The trail bed will now be completely level and straight, with a stone wall on either side of this access road. Walk through an overgrown meadow, and in this vicinity, you'll see ample evidence that this land was once farmland, due to an old cellar hole nearby to your left and stone walls crisscrossing through the woods.

Turn right (west) behind a brown metal gate after passing the 1.8-mile mark, onto the White Trail, a flat and grassy access road. It's not readily apparent that this is a white-blazed trail since markings aren't visible.

Soon you'll be making a steady descent at a slight pitch. Reach a clearing at about 2.0 miles, where you'll see open patches of sky, before heading back into the woods, with some locust trees added to the mix. At about 2.3 miles turn right (west) down a trail spur to explore the canoe campsite and the Pawcatuck River. When you're finished, return to the main trail and continue southwest through dense brush and then into towering pine groves.

It's extremely easy to miss your next turn at 2.4 miles, which is a sharp left (east/45 degrees) breaking away from the access road onto a footpath that continues through towering pine and small oak. White blazes are very faint at first but become bolder and more frequent as you progress farther into the woods, which soon transitions to wooded marsh. Depending on the season and precipitation, portions of this stretch can be extremely muddy, so use caution. The most pronounced of these areas is located at 2.6 miles, before heading into a drier but still low-lying area of beech, oak, and swamp maple.

Cross a brook over a small square stepping-stone and continue on a trail surface alternating between low-lying wooded marsh and slightly elevated woods hosting some rock outcroppings. At 3.0 miles pass through a stone wall; then bear left, not right as this is a herd path. Then at about 3.1 miles turn right (northeast) onto a sandy wood road, continuing on the White Trail.

Buckeye Brook passes under the trail at 3.4 miles, as you continue making a long, gradual climb before leveling out on the sandy access road. As soon as stone walls on either side of the route become visible, you'll begin a steady descent that continues all the way back to the point where you complete the loop, at the next intersection. Turn right (south) here and retrace your steps back to the car.

Miles and Directions

0.0   Begin behind a brown metal gate on a level wood road.

0.3   Continue to the right (north) at the Y intersection, following the Blue Trail.

0.6   Continue straight (north) on the Blue Trail at the junction.

0.8   Pass another junction continuing on the Blue Trail (north).

1.6   Break away from the Blue Trail, making a sharp left (southwest) turn.

1.8   Turn right (west) behind a brown metal gate onto the White Trail.

2.0   Pass through a clearing.

2.3   Turn right (west) down a trail spur to the canoe camp and Pawcatuck River. Return to this junction when you are through and continue southwest.

2.4   Turn sharply left (east) onto a footpath.

2.6   Pass through wooded marsh and over a wet trail surface.

Burlingame North Management Area

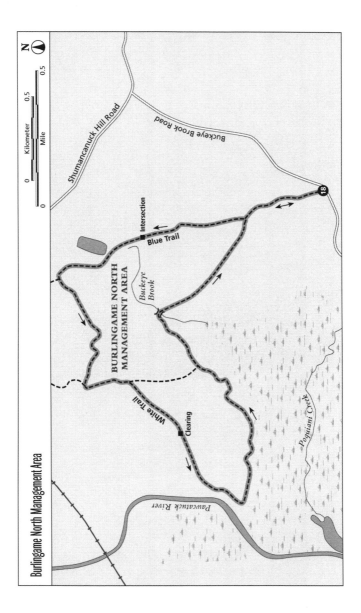

BURLINGAME NORTH MANAGEMENT AREA

Shumancanuck Hill Road

Buckeye Brook Road

Intersection

Blue Trail

Buckeye Brook

White Trail

Clearing

Pawcatuck River

Pequani Creek

18

N

Kilometer   0   0.5

Mile   0   0.5

3.0 Pass through a stone wall and bear left, not right as this is a herd path.

3.1 Turn right (northeast) onto a wood road, continuing on the White Trail.

3.4 Cross Buckeye Brook and begin a long, gradual climb.

4.2 Return to your car.

19 Trustom Pond National Wildlife Refuge

A wide-open meadow directly behind the visitor center in this national wildlife refuge gives way to coastal woodland before surprising you with two peninsulas jutting out into Trustom Pond, narrowly separated by barrier beach from the ocean. Well-marked and maintained trail surfaces, multiple viewing platforms, and plenty of benches make this hike enjoyable and easy to navigate.

Distance: 2.5-mile loop
Approximate hiking time: 1.5 hours
Difficulty: Easy
Elevation gain: 26 feet
Trail surface: Stone-dust footpaths
Best season: Apr–Oct
Other trail users: Bird-watchers
Canine compatibility: No dogs permitted

Permits and fees: None
Schedule: Open year-round sunrise to sunset
Maps: TOPO! New England; map on trailhead signboard
Trail contact: Rhode Island National Wildlife Refuge, U.S. Fish & Wildlife Service, 50 Bend Rd., Charlestown, RI 02813; (401) 364-9124; https://www.fws.gov/refuge/trustom_pond

Finding the trailhead: Located on the state's southern shoreline east of Charlestown, take the Moonstone Beach Road exit from Route 1 (northbound or southbound). Follow Moonstone Beach Road 1 mile south to Matunuck Schoolhouse Road and turn right (west). Follow Matunuck Schoolhouse Road for 0.7 mile to the refuge entrance on the left (south). Trailhead facilities include water, restrooms, and a visitor center.

The Hike

As you stand in the medium-size asphalt parking lot look-ing toward the small visitor center and trailhead, you'll see bathroom facilities and a water fountain across the lot to your left (east). The trail begins on a wooden walkway/deck that abuts the visitor center's right-hand side, leading you to a stone-dust footpath.

You'll immediately see an extensive signboard containing a detailed trail map and information about national wildlife refuges across the United States. Continue on a stone-dust path passing through thick brush that's cleared back about 6 feet on either side of the trail. Much of the land in this refuge used to be part of a working farm.

Turn right at 0.1 mile, which is a well-marked intersec-tion. Brown signs with white lettering indicate that the Otter Point Trail is to your left (east) and Osprey Point Trail is to the right (west). Follow the Osprey Point Trail south, close to the right edge of a large field that's undergoing habitat res-toration, reestablishing native grasses like blue stem, switch, and Indian that were squeezed out by invasive species over the years.

The trail surface transitions to mown grass until you reach another intersection in the upper-right-hand corner of the field at 0.2 mile. Turn right (south) here, into the woods on a sandy wood road leading out to Osprey Point. You'll be passing through a mix of oak, beech, and some holly with little to no coniferous trees. Even though you're passing through a wooded patch, you'll see stone walls, grass growing on the trail surface as well as in patches under many of the trees, and an overgrown meadow to your right suggesting once-upon-a-time farming activity.

The road is grassy and flat, passing through oak ranging from scrub to massive trees growing within underbrush that's cut back on either side of the trail bed, lending it a wood lane ambiance. Benches are interspersed along the trail for nature watching and relaxing. Continue straight out to Osprey Point at 0.7 mile, at another well-marked intersection. You'll hear ocean waves in the distance as you progress on the stone-dust trail heading south. Almost immediately to the left (east), you'll catch a quick view of Trustom Pond, and soon water will be visible through trees on both sides of the trail as the peninsula narrows. A lookout platform at 0.9 mile, complete with viewing telescope, allows you to view the water life right in front of you, as well as in the coves on either side, surrounded by marsh grass.

From the viewing platform, retrace your steps back to the last intersection and turn right (northeast) onto the Red Maple Swamp Trail. Both sides of the sandy grass-covered trail bed are well mown, keeping the thick underbrush bursting with grape vines and briars at bay. The pond is close by to your right (east), even though you can't see it.

As you continue, small cherry and oak poke above the brush, and 1.3 miles marks a spot with another bench to your right (east), facing an extremely wide swamp maple with branches extending great distances in every direction. Wild grass growing underneath the twisting outstretched limbs of this tree makes it a contemplative resting area. Shortly after passing this tree, you'll see an overgrown field through the trees to your right, and then pass through another overgrown field before reaching a Y intersection with an old metal windmill shrouded by trees just beyond to your right (east) at 1.5 miles. Bear right to get a closer look at the windmill. Backed by a stone wall and old wooden fence, it's the perfect reminder that agriculture once predominated here. Afterward, continue back along the main trail.

You'll cross a wooden bridge over a little stream and swampy area at 1.6 miles. Shortly after crossing, you'll see another overgrown field off to the right and then reach a T intersection. Turn right (east), following the trail sign out to Otter Point, the second peninsula you'll explore on this route. Begin by passing down a straight and flat stone-dust path surrounded by alternating overgrown meadow and wooded marsh. You'll see water on either side at 1.9 miles as you're progressing to the point. A wood-planked walkway leads out to an observation platform to your left. The trail continues a little beyond this platform, dead-ending at the water's edge.

Retrace your steps to the junction, continuing straight (north) on the stone-dust path through the intersection. You'll see a bench to your right and a field up ahead through the trees. The trail skirts the edge of the field, providing wide-open meadow views to your left (west). Down below to your right (east), you'll see a pond filled with lily pads. You'll have the opportunity to check out what was once a farm pond using two platforms extending over the water for close-up views.

Upon reaching the second viewing platform, the trail makes a sharp left (west) turn, curving through the center of the field on a stone-dust surface. Continue on the trail to complete the loop at the intersection behind the visitor center. Turn right (north) here and retrace your steps back to the parking lot.

Miles and Directions

0.0 Begin alongside the visitor center.

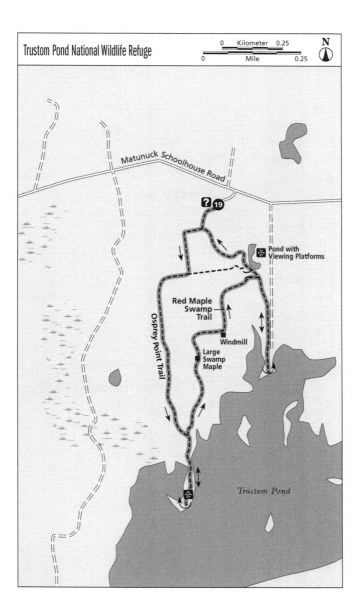

Trustom Pond National Wildlife Refuge

Matunuck Schoolhouse Road

? **19**

Pond with
Viewing Platforms

Red Maple
Swamp
Trail

Osprey Point Trail

Windmill

Large
Swamp
Maple

Trustom Pond

0   Kilometer   0.25

0   Mile   0.25

N

0.1 Turn right (west) at a well-marked intersection toward Osprey Point Trail.

0.2 Turn right (south) on a wood road leading out to Osprey Point.

0.7 Continue straight (south) through the intersection toward the point.

0.9 Enjoy a lookout platform complete with viewing telescope.

1.3 Pass a bench at a huge swamp maple.

1.5 Pass an old metal windmill.

1.6 Cross a wooden bridge over a little stream and swampy area.

1.9 Make your way out to Otter Point.

2.5 Return to your car.

20 Rodman Hollow

Thanks to the Nature Conservancy, 42 percent of Block Island is preserved as open space. In addition to land preserves, many acres are kept free from development through easements with private property owners. The Rodman Hollow loop covers the whole range of terrain that Block Island has to offer, including rolling meadow, grand Atlantic Ocean views, and a rare instance of being surrounded by a relatively mature forest.

Distance: 2.5-mile loop
Approximate hiking time: 2 hours
Difficulty: Moderate
Elevation gain: 119 feet
Trail surface: Sand and gravel access roads, footpaths
Best season: Apr–Oct
Other trail users: Bird-watchers, horseback riders
Canine compatibility: No dogs permitted

Permits and fees: None
Schedule: Open year-round sunrise to sunset
Maps: TOPO! New England and www.natureblockisland.org/trails-on-block-island
Trail contact: The Nature Conservancy, Rhode Island Chapter, 159 Waterman St., Providence, RI 02906; (401) 331-7110 or the Block Island Office at (401) 466-2129; ri@tnc.org

Finding the trailhead: To reach the trailhead, you'll either have to rent a bike on Block Island or bring your own. Trailhead is about 3 miles from ferry landing, which will take about a half hour by bike. From the ferry terminal, turn right and pedal down Water Street, which curves sharply to the left (west) to become Dodge Street and then Ocean Avenue at the intersection with Corn Neck/Old Town Roads. Continue across Beach Avenue (kitty-corner right then left) onto West Side Road. Follow West Side Road up a long series of hills until it curves left (east) sharply into Cooneymus Road. The trailhead is approximately 0.25 mile up Cooneymus Road to your right (south), well marked with signage.

The Hike

The trail begins on a sand-rutted stone access road off Cooneymus Road. Walk past a signboard to your right before passing around a green metal gate. Head down a hill surrounded by underbrush, and you'll pass a small wooden sign to your right after about 100 feet indicating that you're passing Old Mill Road, a grassy access road. Continue straight (south) down the rutted and twisting road ahead.

Soon you'll notice a stone wall close by to your left (east) with a field behind it visible through the underbrush. After this initial descent, the wood road levels out to a sandy flat grade surrounded by brushy wooded marsh to your right (west). You'll pass an intersection with a trail off to your left at 0.2 mile, fronted by a wooden fence and turnstile to prevent mountain bikes from gaining access. Continue straight (south) and shortly the trail will open up into a wide meadow that's relatively flat off to your right and rolls upward gradually to your left.

At 0.4 mile you'll reach a good vantage point within the field where, to your right (west), you can see birdhouses clustered up on a hill, along with a marsh pond visible through meadow grass and dense underbrush. To your left are rolling fields with tall trees towering as a backdrop. Another vantage point at 0.7 mile reveals the ocean in the distance, and to your right rolling meadow gives way to views of the rooftops of houses up on a ridge.

At 0.8 mile pass straight through a four-way intersection; then reach a T intersection at about 0.9 mile with a trail that follows the oceanside bluff to your right (west) and left (east). Turn left (east) and parallel the ocean view to your right (south), enjoying some good overlooks featuring the bluff's gray clay contrasting with the bright blue ocean crashing on darker seaweed-encrusted rocks below. Looking up to the left at the rolling meadows completes the scene.

At about the 1.0-mile mark you will encounter a four-way intersection. To the left, a wide access road departs up the hill. To the right is yet another overlook with the wide Atlantic spreading before you. Go straight to continue paralleling the ocean, careful not to wander to close to the cliff edge as this ground is unstable, though the trail maintains a safe distance from the edge. The trail narrows then opens onto a field to your left (north), the ocean to your right (south), and the trail winding along the field's edge (east). Soon you'll come to a granite bench at an overlook that offers a magnificent view of the Block Island coast and broad Atlantic. Follow the trail as it bends along the edge of the field.

At about 1.1 miles you will reconnect with the access road you'd crossed moments before. Turn right (northeast) and follow until you see a trail diverting to the left (north) marked by a small sign, JONES TRAIL. Take this trail, climbing up through underbrush. After a brief span, you'll pass larger pines that appear to be dead or dying with some that have portions that are still alive. Steadily climb up and then through a grove of the dead taller pines clustered up on the hillside. You'll experience the first shade on the route under cover of these half-dead evergreens, cedars, and medium-size locusts.

The trail bed twists and turns with sharp curves up until the 1.4-mile mark where you'll depart the cover of light woods into more open underbrush without any trees. At 1.5 miles, a trail departs to the left (northwest); go straight. Continue straight through a grassy clearing along a wide grass-covered footpath.

Soon you'll reach another grassy clearing marked with a line of stones running perpendicular to the trail. From here you'll see wide-open rolling meadows and houses in the distance. You'll continue to noticeably lose elevation then climb some steep portions of trail through underbrush cleared back from either side of the trail.

Turn right (northeast) at 1.7 miles, which marks another T intersection, continuing on an ample grassy lane. Soon, you'll suddenly head down a steep hill into a tunnel of underbrush at about 1.8 miles marking the beginning of Rodman Hollow. The trail surface by now has transitioned to a rugged rocky footpath.

At 1.9 miles you'll pass a wooden sign pointing to FRESH POND to your right (east). Continue straight (northwest) and begin a long and steady climb through wooded terrain.

You'll finally level out once you pass a well-formed stone wall immediately to your left (north) continuing to parallel to trail for a bit. After winding farther, at 2.3 miles turn right at a T intersection up toward the wooden fence with a turnstile that you passed at the beginning of the route. Upon reaching the turnstile, complete the loop by retracing your steps back to the trailhead.

Miles and Directions

0.0 Begin behind a green metal gate.

0.1 Pass a small wooden sign indicating that you're passing Old Mill Road.

0.2 Continue straight (south) past a wooden fence and turnstile.

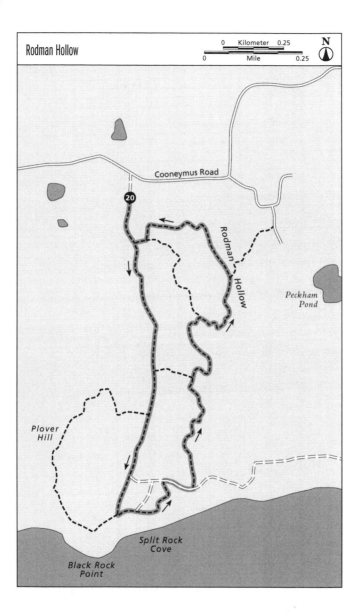

Rodman Hollow

Cooneymus Road

20

Rodman Hollow

Peckham Pond

Plover Hill

Split Rock Cove

Black Rock Point

0.4 Pass a good vantage point within a field.

0.7 Enjoy another vantage point with ocean views.

0.9 Turn left (east) at a T intersection high on a bluff and parallel the ocean.

1.0 Continue through a four-way intersection to follow the trail up the bluff to an overlook with a granite bench. Follow along the edge of the field.

1.1 Reconnect with the access road and turn right (northeast).

1.2 Turn left onto a narrow trail marked with a small sign, JONES TRAIL.

1.4 Depart the cover of light woods; then continue straight (north) through a grassy intersection.

1.7 Turn right (northeast) at a T intersection and head into Rodman Hollow.

2.3 Turn right at a T intersection, walking toward the wooden turnstile you passed earlier.

2.5 Return to the parking area and your bike.

THE TEN ESSENTIALS OF HIKING

American Hiking Society

Whether you plan to be gone for a couple of hours or several months, make sure to pack these items. Become familiar with these items and know how to use them.

Find other helpful resources at AmericanHiking.org/hiking-resources

1. **Appropriate Footwear**

2. **Navigation**

3. **Water** (and a way to purify it)

4. **Food**

5. **Rain Gear & Dry-Fast Layers**

6. **Safety Items** (light, fire, and a whistle)

7. **First Aid Kit**

8. **Knife or Multi-Tool**

9. **Sun Protection**

10. **Shelter**